SECOND EDITION

AIMR PERFORMANCE PRESENTATION STANDARDS HANDBOOK

1997

**AIMR** Association for
Investment Management
and Research

To obtain the AIMR *Publications Catalog*, contact:
AIMR, P.O. Box 3668, Charlottesville, Virginia 22903, U.S.A.
Phone 804-980-3668; Fax 804-977-1103; E-mail info@aimr.com or
visit AIMR's World Wide Web site at
http://www.aimr.org
to view the AIMR publications list.

Updates to the Standards, including committee reports, interpretations,
and most frequently asked questions and answers, will be published in
AIMR's *Standards Reporter*. For more information on the *Standards
Reporter*, please contact AIMR at 804-980-3668.

ISBN 1-879087-78-2
Printed in the United States of America
November 1996

Contents

Foreword

The AIMR Performance Presentation Standards were first introduced by the Financial Analysts Federation's Committee for Performance Presentation Standards in the September/October 1987 issue of the *Financial Analysts Journal*. Since that time, the AIMR-PPS™ standards have been reviewed extensively by members of the industry and revised in response to their many comments and recommendations. The underlying principles, however, have remained the same.

In 1990, the AIMR Board of Governors endorsed the AIMR-PPS standards and approved the establishment of the Performance Presentation Standards Implementation Committee to review the Standards and seek industry input prior to formal implementation in 1993. The Implementation Committee continues to operate as a standing AIMR committee with the responsibilities of reviewing the Standards as the industry evolves, providing interpretation and clarification of the Standards, and expanding the principles of the Standards as new situations warrant. AIMR recognizes its responsibility to review the Standards on an ongoing basis so that the Standards remain relevant to the changing characteristics of the global investment industry.

The original AIMR-PPS standards have been revised—and supplementary material added—as a result of the work of the Implementation Committee and its various subcommittees. (Appendix E contains a list of committee and subcommittee members.) Several subcommittees have studied issues specific to application of the Standards in areas outside the scope of the original Standards, such as international investing, the treatment of portfolios using leverage and/or derivatives, real estate, bank trust departments, venture capital and private placements, wrap-fee portfolios, the calculation of after-tax returns, and verification. This publication incorporates the dedicated work of these committees.

In 1995, AIMR formed the Global PPS Subcommittee to further address international performance issues and to develop global standards for presenting investment performance. Outside of North America, the Swiss Bankers Association has adopted standards virtually identical to the AIMR-PPS standards. Other countries are also considering adopting similar performance presentation standards. AIMR anticipates that increasing global interest in the Standards and the development of Global Performance Presentation Standards will continue.

The original Financial Analysts Federation Committee for Performance Presentation Standards was established at the request of Frederick L. (Ted) Muller, CFA, Atlanta Capital Management Company, who at the time was chair of the FAF, and was chaired by Claude N. Rosenberg, Jr., RCM Capital Management. Other committee members included R.H. Jeffrey, The Jeffrey Company; Robert G. Kirby, Capital Guardian Trust Group; Dean LeBaron, CFA, Batterymarch Financial Management; and John J.F. Sherrerd, CFA, Miller, Anderson & Sherrerd.

AIMR's Performance Presentation Standards Implementation Committee began its efforts under the leadership of Ted Muller, the committee's initial chair, and continues its work today under its current co-chairs, Lee N. Price, CFA, RCM Capital Management, and R. Charles Tschampion, CFA, General Motors Investment Management Corporation. AIMR is indebted to these outstanding professionals and to all past and present committee members, AIMR members, investment professionals, AIMR staff, and others who made invaluable contributions to the AIMR-PPS standards. Special recognition is given to Ted Muller; his vision and dedication are what have enabled the Standards to be so widely accepted today.

From all involved in the creation of the second edition, we hope you find the *AIMR Performance Presentation Standards Handbook* useful and informative.

Michael S. Caccese, Esq.
Senior Vice President,
General Counsel, and
Secretary
Association for Investment Management and Research

Preface to the Second Edition

The second edition of the *AIMR Performance Presentation Standards Handbook* contains much of the same information as the first edition, but the organization has been changed to make the material easier to use and understand. This section summarizes aspects of the new structure and some of the substantive changes to be found in the second edition. Readers of the *Handbook* should not rely on this section as the only source for changes to the AIMR-PPS standards but should look at the revised Standards anew and in their entirety.

Following the Introduction section, the AIMR Performance Presentation Standards are stated in their entirety. All of the requirements and recommendations of the Standards are set forth in this Statement of the Performance Presentation Standards. Note that AIMR strongly encourages that the Standards listed as recommendations also be adopted and implemented, in accordance with the spirit and intent of the AIMR-PPS standards.

The requirements and recommendations sections of the Statement and the five chapters of this edition are organized into five main topics:

- Creation and Maintenance of Composites,
- Calculation of Returns,
- Presentation of Results,
- Disclosures, and
- Verification (recommendations only).

The AIMR-PPS standards have been grouped in these categories and stated together to enhance the reader's ability to understand and apply the Standards. At the beginning of each chapter, the requirements and recommendations relating to the topic are restated for ease of reference, and each chapter provides a detailed discussion of the topic.

The chapter discussions incorporate not only the detailed information previously included in both the body and the appendixes of the 1993 *Performance Presentation Standards* handbook but also relevant substantive material from the subcommittee reports. For example, the requirements and recommendations regarding such specific areas as international investing, taxable accounts, real estate, venture and private placements, and wrap-fee accounts are discussed in each topical chapter.

The second edition has been organized in this way so as to locate the discussion regarding each major topic in one place in the book.

For example, a reader wanting more discussion on the requirements and recommendations regarding the disclosures specific to real estate can simply turn to the real estate subheading in Chapter 4 to obtain that information. Following the chapters, Appendixes A–D provide specific examples, models, and sample presentations.

Some of the substantive overall changes found in the new *Handbook* include the following:

New Requirements

Changes in definition of a "firm." The AIMR-PPS standards now allow a firm to be defined as "an autonomous investment firm, subsidiary, or division held out to the public as a separate entity" even if it is not actually a separate legal entity. This expanded definition of the firm has been added in an effort to encourage more banks and other entities to come into compliance with the Standards and also to allow the Standards to gain continued global acceptance. In recognition of this additional definition, a new *required disclosure* has been added: The firm must state exactly how it is defining itself for purposes of compliance with the Standards. The Standards state that the same definition of the firm must be used in the calculation of "firm assets" for marketing purposes as is used in the standard presentation format that shows the size of each composite relative to total firm assets. Claiming compliance for all of a firm's assets managed with respect to any given base currency will continue to be possible. In defining the firm entity, firms need to keep in mind the spirit and full intent of the Standards, namely, fair representation and full disclosure.

Performance history must include a measure of composite dispersion. Presentations of annual performance history are now required to include a measure of composite dispersion for each year. This stipulation has been upgraded, from being a recommendation in the first edition, because the Implementation Committee believes that a measure of composite dispersion (previously referred to as "internal risk") is so important to the clients' understanding of past performance that it must be mandatory in the presentation of annual results.

The Standards include a new Compliance Statement. The new statement is as follows:

[Insert firm name] has prepared and presented this report in compliance with the Performance Presentation Standards of the Association for Investment Management and Research (AIMR-PPS™). AIMR has not been involved with the preparation or review of this report.

The Compliance Statement may be used only after every reasonable effort has been made to ensure that the performance presentation is in compliance with the AIMR-PPS standards. This change is to standardize the claim of compliance for industrywide recognition.

◼ *Inclusion of accrued income in market values.* The definition of beginning and ending market values in performance calculations must include accrued income. Although the distinction is fairly technical, some firms have included accrued income in the numerator for performance calculations but not in the denominator, thus overstating fixed-income performance in most situations. In other words, accrued income must be included in both the numerator and the denominator for performance calculations. This change will ensure that the goal of fair representation is met in the presentation of performance results.

New Recommendations

◼ *Encourage more frequent, ideally daily, portfolio valuations.* The AIMR-PPS standards encourage frequent portfolio valuation, ideally daily valuation with geometric linking. More frequent portfolio valuations provide a more accurate representation of portfolio value, which is in keeping with the full intent of the Standards.

◼ *Verification guidelines.* Guidelines for verification have been added to the recommendations, with the noted requirement that *if a verification is performed*, the verifier must state whether a Level I or Level II verification was performed in order to protect the interests of all parties. It is acceptable to make the Level I or Level II statement in a footnote on the verification report. If verification is undertaken, it must be performed by a third party. Without the statement of Level I or Level II verification, the firm cannot claim that its investment performance has been verified.

◼ *Use temporary accounts for significant cash flows.* The revised AIMR-PPS standards suggest that accounts with significant cash flows (into or out of portfolios) should treat these cash flows as temporary "new" accounts. This recommendation should reduce the tendency of some managers to move accounts into and out of "discretionary" status as a result of large cash flows. Temporary accounts obviate the rationale for moving accounts to nondiscretionary status, an action that should be discouraged because of its potential for abuse. This recommendation is in keeping with the goal of fair representation.

◼ *Use of multiple composites where necessary.* This edition contains more descriptive material than the first edition about balanced composites. It includes the specific recommendation that managers whose balanced accounts differ significantly in allowed range of asset mix should use several balanced composites, rather than a single composite, to provide a fuller representation of composite results.

■ *Computing performance after fees when the manager is paid on a performance-fee basis.* The AIMR-PPS standards include a new standardized method for computing performance after fees when the manager is paid on a performance-fee basis. Because the presentation of performance after fees remains optional (but is recommended), this new method is not mandatory, but the method should help standardize how firms respond to the somewhat complicated process of reporting performance in fee-for-performance situations.

Introduction

Welcome to the AIMR Performance Presentation Standards. This Introduction to the *Handbook* provides an overview of key elements of the AIMR-PPS standards presented in the next section.

The investment community's need for a common, accepted set of guidelines to promote fair representation and full disclosure in every firm's presentation of its performance results to clients and prospective clients has guided the development of the AIMR-PPS standards. The Standards are the manifestation of a set of guiding ethical principles and should be interpreted as *minimum* standards for presenting investment performance. The Standards have been designed to meet the following four goals:

* achieve greater uniformity and comparability among performance presentations;
* improve the service offered to investment management clients;
* enhance the professionalism of the industry;
* bolster the notion of self-regulation.

The Standards set expectations and provide an industry yardstick for evaluating fairness and accuracy in investment performance presentation.

Some aspects of the AIMR-PPS standards are mandatory (i.e., they *must* be followed to claim compliance); other aspects are recommended (i.e., they *should* be followed). Note that AIMR strongly encourages firms to adopt the recommended Standards in addition to the required Standards. Note also that, although the Standards specify minimum calculation requirements, they are intended primarily to be performance *presentation* standards, not performance *measurement* standards. The Standards are neither envisioned nor intended to enhance or detract from the potential value or usefulness of the information contained in historical results.

No finite set of guidelines can cover all potential situations or anticipate future developments in industry structure, technology, or practices. Meeting the objectives of fair representation and full disclosure requires a conscientious, good-faith commitment on the part of the presenter to adhere to the spirit of the AIMR-PPS standards under specific circumstances. Meeting the full intent of the Standards may, and probably will, require *more* than meeting the minimum requirements. Presenters have the responsibility to include disclosures that contain material information not covered in the Standards. No portion of the Standards should be interpreted as inhibiting managers from providing supplemental information requested by prospective clients or consultants or information that would clarify the firm's investment results.

Parties Affected by the Standards

Firms. The AIMR-PPS standards are voluntary standards for the industry. Firms are not required to comply with the Standards when presenting performance, but the Standards are widely recognized as the most effective guidelines for fair and accurate reporting of investment performance.

AIMR Members, CFA Charterholders, and CFA Candidates. Although the AIMR-PPS standards are not explicitly incorporated in the AIMR Code of Ethics and Standards of Professional Conduct, members, charterholders, and candidates may rely upon the AIMR-PPS standards to help ensure that they make no material misrepresentations regarding their performance and that they thereby remain in compliance with the Code of Ethics and Standard V(B), Performance Presentation, of AIMR's Standards of Professional Conduct.[1] Members, charterholders, and candidates are encouraged to inform their employers of the AIMR-PPS standards and to encourage their employers to adopt the Standards.

Prospective and Current Clients. The primary beneficiaries of the AIMR-PPS standards are prospective clients of investment management firms who are attempting to compare the investment performance of these firms. Current clients attempting to evaluate their managers' performance also benefit from the Standards. However, compliance with the Standards does not obviate the need for due diligence on the part of prospective or current clients or consultants in evaluating performance data.

Definition of a Firm

To claim compliance with the AIMR-PPS standards, the firm must comply with the Standards on a firmwide basis. Additionally, the firm must state exactly how it is defining itself for purposes of compliance. The Standards define a firm as

- an entity registered with the appropriate regulatory authority overseeing its investment management activities *or*

---

[1]See the seventh edition of the *Standards of Practice Handbook* (Charlottesville, VA: AIMR, 1996).

- an autonomous investment firm, subsidiary, or division held out to the public as a separate entity (for example, a subsidiary firm may claim compliance for itself without its parent organization being in compliance) *or*
- (for firms managing international assets) all assets managed to one or more base currencies. For example, a firm entity could be defined as all of the assets of a firm managed for clients whose base currency is the U.S. dollar. For firm entities defined as such, all assets managed to the selected base currency must be included and presented in composites that meet compliance requirements. In this example, both discretionary and nondiscretionary U.S. dollar-based assets would be included in the "total firm assets."

Definition of Total Firm Assets

Total firm assets are defined to include all discretionary and non-discretionary assets. "Total firm assets" does not refer to assets underlying overlay investment strategies, such as currency overlays, options and futures overlays, securities lending programs, and asset allocation overlay strategies, *unless* the firm actually manages the underlying assets. Similarly, assets assigned to subadvisors that are not part of the firm are not to be included in total firm assets, and their performance record is, therefore, not part of the firm's record. If the manager has discretion over the underlying assets, those assets are to be included in total firm assets.

Assets to which the AIMR-PPS standards cannot be applied are not to be considered by firms when claiming compliance with the Standards. For example, traditional guaranteed investment contract (GIC) portfolios provide stable results that are not based on a mark-to-market valuation. The valuation of the traditional GIC is based on book value, not current market value, which is the valuation required by the total return calculation and reporting requirements of the Standards. Accordingly, unless the assets in these portfolios are separately marked to market, the portfolio results cannot be reported as being in compliance with the Standards. GIC assets would be reported separately (i.e., not included in the statistic "total firm assets").

Firms managing both traditional GIC and other assets are exempt from reporting the GIC assets in compliance with the AIMR-PPS standards. These firms may claim compliance for the remaining assets. Performance reports for managed GICs and other nontraditional GIC strategies that meet the requirements of total return and market valuation must adhere to the requirements of the Standards in order for the firm to claim compliance.

For the defined firm, all fee-paying accounts with investment discretion must be included in one or more composites. The account portfolios must be grouped into composites based on similar investment strategy or objective. Compliance cannot be met on a per composite or per product basis but can only be met on a firmwide basis. Composites may not be presented as being in compliance unless *all* of the firm's qualifying portfolios have been accounted for in at least one composite defined according to similar strategy or investment objective.

Systems incompatibilities cannot be used as a reason for not claiming compliance for all assets (i.e., a firm cannot make the claim of compliance for only those assets that are measured and monitored on compatible systems).

Firms with investment assets under management that adhere to all the required elements of the AIMR-PPS standards when presenting their performance record may claim compliance with the Standards. Plan sponsors, consultants, and software vendors, on the other hand, cannot make a claim of compliance unless these entities *actually manage* the assets for which they are making the claim of compliance. These groups can claim to *endorse* the Standards and/ or *require* that the investment management firms they employ, from which they solicit information, or to which they sell be in compliance with the Standards.

Effective Dates for Compliance

For an investment firm to claim compliance with the AIMR-PPS standards, the firm must meet the following effective dates:

- From January 1, 1993, going forward, all of the firm's actual discretionary fee-paying nontaxable portfolios solely invested in U.S. and/or Canadian investments ("North American portfolios") must be presented in composites that adhere to the Standards.
- From January 1, 1994, going forward, all of the firm's actual discretionary fee-paying portfolios invested in non-U.S. and/or non-Canadian investments ("international portfolios") and taxable portfolios (both North American and international) must be presented in composites that adhere to the Standards.
- From July 1, 1995, going forward, all of the firm's actual discretionary fee-paying portfolios meeting the definition of a wrap-fee account must be presented in composites that adhere to the Standards.

- From January 1, 1997, going forward, all of the firm's composites and performance presentations must include accrued income in market value performance calculations. In addition, *all* of the firm's performance presentations, including presentations of historical performance, must contain a measure of composite dispersion.

The effective dates of firm compliance for North American nontaxable, taxable, international, and wrap-fee accounts must be disclosed. The term "international" portfolios, as referenced in the AIMR-PPS standards, means any non-U.S. or non-Canadian assets or portfolios. For purposes of the Standards, the definition of a wrap account is the same as the U. S. Securities and Exchange Commission's definition of a wrap-fee program. The wrap-fee definition currently reads as follows:

> a program [account] under which any client is charged a specified fee or fees not based directly upon transactions in a client's account for investment advisory services (which may include portfolio management or advice concerning the selection of other investment advisers) and execution of client transactions.

Based on the AIMR–Swiss Bankers Association Reciprocity Agreement, Swiss firms may come into compliance with the AIMR-PPS standards effective January 1, 1997, by adopting all the applicable provisions of the Swiss Bankers Association (SBA) Swiss Performance Presentation Standards. The same provision for definition of a firm as outlined by the AIMR-PPS standards applies for Swiss firms in this situation. Firms in compliance with the SBA Standards can concurrently claim compliance with the AIMR Standards and shall use the following claim of compliance for dual AIMR/SBA compliance:

> [Insert firm name] has prepared and presented this report in compliance with the Performance Presentation Standards of the Association for Investment Management and Research pursuant to the Swiss Bankers Association's Swiss Performance Presentation Standards with an effective compliance date of January 1, 1997. AIMR and the SBA have not been involved with the preparation or review of this report.

Retroactive Compliance

The AIMR-PPS standards require that firms report, at a minimum, 10 years of investment performance (or performance since the inception of the firm if inception is less than 10 years) to claim compliance with the Standards.

Firms with records or performance calculations for periods prior to the applicable effective date(s) that are not in conformance with the AIMR-PPS standards can still claim compliance with the Standards *if certain conditions are met.* To claim compliance, such a firm has three options:

- restate its historical performance numbers in accordance with the Standards,
- restate its historical performance in accordance with the Relaxed Retroactive Standards, explained in the following paragraph, for retroactive compliance, or
- use its nonconforming historical performance and disclose specifically when and how the performance is not in compliance.

The first option is the desired approach. For the second option, under the Relaxed Retroactive Standards for compliance prior to January 1, 1993, two relaxations are allowed:

- Portfolios and composites may be valued on an annual basis as a maximum. Valuation periods for both portfolios and composites may be as long as one year (although if cash flows were significant during the year, valuations should be done more frequently). To qualify for inclusion in a composite that is valued annually, a portfolio must have been under management according to a strategy appropriate to the composite for at least one year.
- Accrual accounting need not be applied.

For the third option, if a firm claims compliance with the AIMR-PPS standards but the pre-January 1, 1993, historical record is not in compliance for all periods and the noncompliance periods are linked to periods that are in compliance, the firm must

- disclose that the full record is not in compliance,
- identify the noncompliance periods, and
- explain exactly how the noncompliance periods are out of compliance.

Compliance Example with Effective Dates

Firm A was founded on January 1, 1990. Prior to January 1, 1993, the firm made annual valuations, used cash-basis accounting, and did not asset-weight composites. Since January 1, 1993, the performance of all the firm's nontaxable North American portfolios has been presented in conformance with all the AIMR-PPS requirements. Since January 1, 1994, the performance of all the firm's international and taxable portfolios has been presented in compliance with all the Standards requirements. Since July 1, 1995, the performance of all the firm's portfolios subject to wrap fees has been presented in compliance with all the Standards requirements.

Effective January 1, 1996, the firm wants to begin claiming compliance with the AIMR-PPS standards. Generally, firms must be able to present a 10-year performance history to claim compliance. Firm A is less than 10 years old, but it can claim compliance despite the lack of a 10-year history as long as it presents its full record of performance from the date of inception of the firm.

Prior to January 1, 1993, Firm A was not in compliance with the AIMR-PPS standards because the firm used annual valuations as opposed to the required minimum of quarterly valuations, used cash-basis accounting as opposed to accrual accounting, and did not asset-weight composites. To claim compliance, Firm A has the three options:

■ *Option 1.* Firm A can bring its historical performance into compliance by recalculating and restating its performance from January 1, 1990, to January 1, 1993, in *full* compliance with the Standards (i.e., making quarterly valuations, using accrual accounting, and creating asset-weighted composites).

■ *Option 2.* Firm A can apply the Relaxed Retroactive Standards. Firm A can bring its historical performance into compliance by recalculating and restating its performance from January 1, 1990, to January 1, 1993, in compliance with the Relaxed Retroactive Standards. For the period January 1, 1990, to January 1, 1993, Firm A used annual valuations, used cash-basis accounting, and did not asset-weight composites. Under this second option, for Firm A to claim full compliance as of January 1, 1990, the firm must create asset-weighted composites of its portfolios for the 1990–93 time period. Because annual valuations and cash-basis accounting are allowable under the Relaxed Retroactive Standards, the firm would not have to go back and recalculate performance using more frequent valuations or accrual accounting.

■ *Option 3.* Firm A, because it is less than 10 years old, can present its full performance history, claim compliance as of January 1, 1993, and
- disclose that its performance from January 1, 1990, to January 1, 1993, is not in compliance,
- identify the noncompliance periods, and
- explain exactly how its performance prior to January 1, 1993, is not in compliance.

If Firm A does not want to show its performance history prior to 1993 or does not want to disclose that it is not in compliance prior to January 1, 1993, the firm must wait until 2003 to claim compliance. At that time, the firm will have achieved a 10-year history that can be presented in compliance with the AIMR-PPS standards.

If a firm would like to claim compliance but does not have records to substantiate past performance, it can claim compliance if the lack of records for the missing period(s) is disclosed. Lack of records means that the *underlying data* to support the performance record were either never kept or were lost or destroyed because of extreme circumstances beyond the control of the manager (e.g., a natural disaster). For example, if the records of Firm A from inception in 1990 through December 31, 1993, were destroyed under extreme circumstances beyond the control of the manager, the firm can still claim compliance by showing its performance going forward from January 1, 1994, in a form that is in compliance with the AIMR-PPS standards and disclosing that its records for the period from January 1, 1990, through December 31, 1993, were lost.

Claim of Compliance

To claim compliance, firms must meet all composite, calculation, presentation, and disclosure requirements of the AIMR-PPS standards. Firms also are strongly encouraged to follow the recommended Standards.

Strict adherence to the basic requirements does not guarantee fair and adequate performance reporting. The AIMR-PPS requirements may not cover the specific situation of every firm. In preparing performance reports, firms must keep in mind the spirit and objectives of the Standards: fair representation and full disclosure. Meeting the intent of the Standards will likely require actions over and above simple satisfaction of the minimum requirements. Compliance with the Standards also requires adherence to all applicable laws and regulations.

The following legend (i.e., the Compliance Statement) may be used only after every reasonable effort is made to ensure that the performance presentation is in compliance with the AIMR-PPS standards:

> [Insert name of firm] has prepared and presented this report in compliance with the Performance Presentation Standards of the Association for Investment Management and Research (AIMR-PPS™). AIMR has not been involved with the preparation or review of this report.

Any use of the marks "AIMR" or "AIMR-PPS" except as specifically provided in the above legend is prohibited. If results are not in full compliance, performance cannot be presented as being "in compliance with the AIMR-PPS standards except for . . . ." Statements referring to the calculation methodology used in a presentation as being "in accordance (or compliance) with AIMR-PPS standards" are prohibited. For a sample performance presentation incorporating the Compliance Statement, refer to Appendix D.

AIMR members who misuse the terms "AIMR," "AIMR-PPS standards," or the Compliance Statement; misrepresent their performance history; or falsely claim compliance with the Standards are subject to disciplinary sanctions under Standard V(B) of AIMR's Standards of Professional Conduct. Possible disciplinary sanctions include public censure, suspension of membership, and revocation of the Chartered Financial Analyst designation. AIMR will also take appropriate action against any firm that misuses the marks "AIMR," "AIMR-PPS," or the Compliance Statement, including false claims of compliance with the AIMR-PPS standards.

Statement of the

AIMR PERFORMANCE PRESENTATION STANDARDS
AIMR-PPS™

I. REQUIREMENTS

To be in compliance with the AIMR Performance Presentation Standards, a firm's presentation of its investment performance must comply with the following requirements on a *firmwide* basis:

A. Creation and Maintenance of Composites

1. General

   a. All actual fee-paying discretionary portfolios must be included in at least one composite defined according to similar strategy or investment objective.

   b. Composites must include new portfolios at the start of the next performance measurement period (at least quarterly) after the portfolio comes under management or according to reasonable and consistently applied firm guidelines.

   c. Composites must exclude terminated portfolios after the last full performance measurement period the portfolios were under management, but composites must continue to include terminated portfolios for all periods prior to termination.

   d. Portfolios must not be switched from one composite to another unless documented changes in client guidelines make switching appropriate.

   e. Convertible and other hybrid securities must be treated consistently across and within composites.

   f. Asset-only returns must not be mixed with asset-plus-cash returns.

2. International

   Subsectors or carve-outs of larger international composites may be used to create stand-alone composites only if the subsectors are actually managed as separate entities with their own cash allocations and currency management.

3. Venture and Private Placements

    All discretionary pooled funds of funds and separately managed portfolios must be included in composites defined by vintage year (i.e., the year of fund formation and first takedown of capital).

B. Calculation of Returns

1. General

    a. Total return, including realized and unrealized gains plus income, must be used when calculating investment performance.

    b. Time-weighted rates of return must be used.

    c. Accrual accounting must be used for fixed-income and all other securities that accrue income. Accrued income must be included in the market value calculation of the denominator and the numerator.

    d. Composites must be asset weighted using beginning-of-period weightings.

    e. Returns from cash and cash equivalents held in portfolios must be included in return calculations, and the cash and cash equivalents must be included in the portfolio amount (total assets) on which the return is calculated.

    f. Portfolios must be valued at least quarterly, and periodic returns must be geometrically linked.

    g. Performance must be calculated after the deduction of trading expenses (e.g., broker commissions and SEC fees), if any.

    h. When portfolios use leverage to purchase securities, return results must be calculated on both an actual basis and a restated, "all cash" basis. For a composite that consists of externally leveraged and unleveraged accounts (for example, securities on margin), the leveraged accounts must be restated to all cash when the return of the composite is computed.

    i. All documents must be maintained that are necessary to form the basis for or demonstrate the calculation of the performance or rate of return of all managed accounts that the advisor includes in a composite (current and historical performance results).

2. International

   The benchmark for any currency overlay portfolio must be calculated in accordance with the mandate of the portfolio unless the benchmark is actually the currency return on a published benchmark.

3. Taxable Clients

   For after-tax composites:

   a. Taxes must be recognized in the same period as when the taxable event occurred.

   b. Taxes on income and realized capital gains must be subtracted from results regardless of whether taxes are paid from assets outside the account or from account assets.

   c. The maximum federal income tax rates appropriate to the portfolios must be assumed.

   d. The return for after-tax composites that hold both taxable and tax-exempt securities must be adjusted to an after-tax basis rather than being "grossed up" to a taxable equivalent.

   e. Calculation of after-tax returns for tax-exempt bonds must include amortization and accretion of premiums or discounts.

   f. Taxes on income are to be recognized on an accrual basis.

4. Real Estate

   a. Real estate must be valued through an independent appraisal at least once every three years unless client agreements state otherwise.

   b. Real estate valuations must be reviewed at least quarterly.

   c. Component returns for participating or convertible mortgages must be allocated as follows:

      • basic cash interest to income return,
      • contingent interest (current receivable) to income return,
      • basic accrued interest (deferred) to income return,
      • additional contingent interest (deferred; payable at maturity, prepayment, or sale) to appreciation return,

- return that is currently payable from operations to income return, and
- all other sources of income that are deferred or realizable in the future to the appreciation component.

5. Venture and Private Placements

   a. General partners

- Cumulative internal rate of return (IRR) must be presented since inception of the fund and be net of fees, expenses, and carry to the limited partner.
- IRR must be calculated based on cash-on-cash returns plus residual value.

   b. Intermediaries and investment advisors

- For separately managed accounts and commingled fund-of-funds structures, cumulative IRR must be presented since inception of the fund and be net of fees, expenses, and carry to the limited partners but gross of investment advisory fees unless net of fees is required to meet applicable regulatory requirements.
- Calculation of IRR must be based on an aggregation of all the appropriate partnership cash flows into one IRR calculation—as if from one investment.

C. Presentation of Results

1. General

   a. A 10-year performance record (or a record for the period since firm inception if inception is less than 10 years) must be presented.

   b. Annual returns for all years must be presented. Performance for periods of less than one year must not be annualized.

   c. Composite results may not be restated following changes in a firm's organization.

   d. Composites must include only assets under management and may not link simulated or model portfolios with actual performance.

   e. For composites containing portfolios that use leverage:

- If the use of leverage is discretionary, the performance presented must include the effects of the leverage. Performance on a restated, all-cash basis (i.e., removing the effect of the leverage from the return) must also be provided.

- If the use of leverage is nondiscretionary (i.e., mandated by the client), performance must be presented on an all-cash basis.

f. Performance results of a past firm or affiliation must not be used to represent the historical record of a new affiliation or a new firm entity.

2. International

If a stand-alone composite is formed using subsectors from multiple composites, its return must be presented with:

- a list of the underlying composites from which the subsector was drawn *and*
- the percentage of each composite the subsector represents.

3. Real Estate

Returns from income and capital appreciation must be presented in addition to total return.

4. Venture and Private Placements

a. General partners

- Cumulative IRR must be presented since inception of the fund.
- Presentation of return information must be in a vintage-year format.

b. Intermediaries and investment advisors

- For separately managed accounts and commingled fund-of-funds structures, cumulative IRR must be presented since inception.
- The inclusion of all discretionary pooled fund-of-funds and separately managed portfolios in composites must be defined by vintage year.
- For calculating composite returns, the IRR must be based on an aggregation of all the appropriate partnership cash flows into one IRR calculation—as if from one investment.

5. Wrap-Fee Accounts

Wrap-fee performance must be shown net of all fees charged

directly or indirectly to the account (unless transaction expenses can be determined and deducted).

D. Disclosures

To be in compliance with the AIMR-PPS standards, a firm's presentation of its investment performance must disclose the following information:

1. General

   For all composites, a performance presentation must disclose:

   - the availability of a complete list and description of the firm's composites,
   - the number of portfolios and amount of assets in a composite and the percentage of the firm's total assets the composite represents,
   - the definition of "firm" used to determine the firm's total assets and firmwide compliance,
   - whether balanced portfolio segments are included in single-asset composites and an explanation of how cash has been allocated among asset segments,
   - whether performance results are calculated gross or net of investment management fees, what the firm's fee schedule is, and for net results, the average weighted management fee,
   - the existence of a minimum asset size below which portfolios are excluded from a composite,
   - a measure of the dispersion of individual component portfolio returns around the aggregate composite return,
   - whether settlement-date valuation is used rather than trade-date valuation,
   - the inclusion of any non-fee-paying portfolios in composites and included in the definition of total firm assets,
   - the use and extent of leverage, including a description of the use, frequency, and characteristics of any derivatives used,
   - a material change in personnel responsible for in-

vestment management,

- the effective date of firm compliance, and
- for historical performance records prior to the applicable effective date,
  - the performance that is not in compliance with the requirements of the AIMR-PPS standards and
  - a description of how noncompliance periods are out of compliance.

2. International

   The performance presentation must disclose:

   - whether composites and benchmarks are presented gross or net of withholding taxes on dividends, interest, and capital gains; if net, the assumed tax rate for both the composite and the benchmark,
   - whether the composite is a subsector of a larger portfolio and, if so, the percentage of the larger portfolio the subsector represents,
   - whether representative portfolios are used in the returns of subsectors shown as supplemental information,
   - for composites managed against specific benchmarks, the percentage of the composites invested in countries or regions not included in the benchmark, and
   - for returns that exclude the effect of currency, whether the returns are presented in local currency and, if so, a statement that the local currency return does not account for interest rate differentials in forward currency exchange rates.

3. Taxable Clients

   The performance presentation must disclose:

   - for composites of taxable portfolios, the composite assets as a percentage of total assets in taxable portfolios (including nondiscretionary assets) managed according to the same strategy for the same type of client,

- the tax rate assumptions if performance results are presented after taxes, and
- both client average and manager average performance if adjustments are made for nondiscretionary cash withdrawals.

4. Real Estate

The performance presentation must disclose:

- the absence of independent appraisals,
- the source of the valuation and the valuation policy,
- total fee structure and its relationship to asset valuation,
- the return formula and accounting policies for such items as capital expenditures, tenant improvements, and leasing commissions,
- the cash distribution and retention policy,
- whether the returns
  - are based on audited operating results,
  - exclude any investment expense that may be paid by the investors, or
  - include interest income from short-term cash investments or other related investments, and
- the cash distribution and retention policies with regard to income earned at the investment level.

5. Venture and Private Placements

a. For general partners, the performance presentation must disclose:

- changes in the general partner since inception of fund,
- type of investment, and
- investment strategy.

b. For intermediaries and investment advisors, the performance presentation must disclose:

- the number of portfolios and funds included in the vintage-year composite,
- composite assets,
- composite assets in each vintage year as a percentage

of total firm assets (discretionary and nondiscretionary committed capital), and

- composite assets in each vintage year as a percentage of total private equity assets.

6. Wrap-Fee Accounts

a. When a firm presents portfolios included in a wrap-fee composite that do not meet the wrap-fee definition, the firm must disclose for each year presented:

- the dollar amount of assets represented *and*
- the fee deducted.

b. When wrap-fee composite returns are presented before fees, the performance presentation must disclose:

- fees,
- investment style, and
- the information that "pure" gross-of-fees return does not include transaction costs.

II. RECOMMENDATIONS

AIMR strongly encourages firms to comply with the following recommendations in addition to the requirements. For a particular firm to adhere fully to the spirit and intent of the AIMR-PPS standards (namely, fair representation and full disclosure in performance presentation), adherence to these recommended Standards could very well be necessary. In situations of doubt, firms should fully disclose any assumptions and apply these recommendations in addition to the requirements as necessary.

A. *Creation and Maintenance of Composites*

1. General

    a. Balanced portfolios should be grouped by allowable range of asset mix.

    b. Accounts with significant cash flows (into or out of portfolios) should treat these cash flows as temporary "new" accounts.

2. International

    For international composites, separate composites should be created for:

    - portfolios that allow currency hedging (versus those that prohibit currency hedging) unless the use of hedging is judged to be immaterial *and*
    - portfolios that are managed against hedged benchmarks (versus those that are managed against unhedged benchmarks).

3. Wrap-Fee Accounts

    Wrap-fee portfolios should be grouped in separate composites from nonwrapped composites.

4. Taxable Clients

    a. Portfolios should be grouped by tax rate.

    b. Portfolios may be grouped by vintage year, or similar proxy, to group portfolios with similar amounts of unrealized capital gains.

B. *Calculation of Returns*

1. General

    a. Equal-weighted composites should be calculated in addition to, but not instead of, asset-weighted composites.

    b.   Accrual accounting for dividends (as of the ex-dividend date) is recommended.

    c.   Accrual accounting for fixed-income securities, although required only after the applicable implementation date, is strongly recommended for *all* performance periods.

    d.   Accrued interest should be included in market value calculations in both the numerator *and* denominator for all periods, although the inclusion is required only after the applicable implementation date.

    e.   Portfolios should be valued on a daily basis or, if not daily, whenever cash flows and market action combine to materially distort performance.

    f.   Trade-date accounting should be used.

2. International

    a.   A consistent source of exchange rates should be used.

    b.   Returns should be calculated net of withholding taxes on dividends, interest, and capital gains.

    c.   Whenever the currency overlay manager is notified of changes in the underlying currency exposures as a result of a shift in the underlying assets, the currency overlay portfolios should be revalued (e.g., for attribution purposes).

3. Taxable Clients

    a.   Cash-basis accounting is to be used if required by applicable law.

    b.   Calculations should be adjusted for nondiscretionary capital gains.

    c.   Benchmark returns should be calculated using the actual turnover in the benchmark index, if available; otherwise, an approximation is acceptable.

    d.   If returns are presented before taxes, a total rate of return for the composite should be presented without adjustment for tax-exempt income to a pretax basis.

4. Real Estate

Income earned at the investment level should be included in the computation of income return regardless of the investor's accounting policies for recognizing income from real estate investments.

5. Venture and Private Placement

   a. General partners

      - Standard industry guidelines should be used for valuation of venture capital investments,

      - valuation should be either cost or discount to comparables in the public market for buyout, mezzanine, distressed, or special situation investments, and

      - IRR should be calculated net of fees, expenses, and carry without public stocks discounted and assuming stock distributions were held.

   b. Net cumulative IRR (after deduction of advisory fees and any other administrative expenses or carried interest) should be calculated for separately managed accounts, managed accounts, and commingled fund-of-funds structures.

C. Presentation of Results

1. General

   a. Composite performance should be presented gross of investment management fees and before taxes (except for international withholding taxes).

   b. Equal-weighted composite results should be presented as supplemental information.

   c. Supplemental information the firm deems valuable should be presented.

2. International

   For presentations of returns excluding currency (e.g., for attribution purposes), local currency returns should be calculated using spot rates and hedged returns should be calculated using forward rates.

3. Taxable Clients

   If returns are presented after taxes, client-specific tax rates may be used for each portfolio (but composite performance should be based on the same tax rate for all clients in the composite). The following presentations should be made for composites:

      - beginning and ending market values,

      - contributions and withdrawals,

- beginning and ending unrealized capital gains,
- realized short-term and long-term capital gains,
- taxable income and tax-exempt income,
- the accounting convention used for the treatment of realized capital gains (e.g., highest cost, average cost, lowest cost, FIFO, LIFO), and
- the method or source for computing after-tax benchmark return (if a benchmark is shown).

4. Real Estate

   a. Equity ownership investment strategies should be presented separately.

   b. When presenting the components of total return, recognition of income at the investment level, rather than at the operating level, is preferred.

5. Wrap-Fee Accounts

   Pure gross-of-fees performance should be reported (in addition to the required net-of-fees performance), but gross-of-fees performance should be presented only to prospective wrap-fee clients.

D. Disclosures

Following are the recommended additional disclosures to fully meet the spirit and intent of fair representation and full disclosure in compliance with the AIMR-PPS standards:

1. General

   For all composites, a performance presentation should disclose:

   a. volatility of the aggregate composite return,

   b. benchmarks that parallel the risk or investment style the composite is expected to track,

   c. differences in portfolio structure relative to the designated benchmarks,

   d. cumulative composite returns for all periods, and

   e. portfolio size range for each composite (unless portfolios are five or fewer) and the percentage of total assets managed in the same asset class as represented by the composite.

2. International

   a. For composites, performance presentation should disclose:

      - the range or the average country weights of a composite that is managed against a specific benchmark and

      - inconsistencies among portfolios within a composite in the treatment of exchange rates.

   b. For presentations of returns excluding the effect of currency (e.g., for attribution purposes), whether the return is the hedged return (using forward rates) or the local return (using spot rates) should be specified. Local returns should be accompanied by a statement that the local return is in local currency and does not account for interest rate differentials in forward currency exchange rates.

3. Venture and Private Placements

   a. For general partners, the following should be disclosed:

      - gross IRR (before fees, expenses, and carry), which should be used at the fund and the portfolio level, as supplemental information,

      - the multiple on committed capital net of fees and carry to the limited partners,

      - the multiple on invested capital gross of fees and carry,

      - the distribution multiple on paid-in capital net of fees to the limited partners, and

      - the residual multiple on paid-in capital net of fees and carry to the limited partners.

   b. Intermediaries and investment advisors

      The number and size should be expressed in terms of committed capital of discretionary and nondiscretionary consulting clients.

E. Verification

The AIMR-PPS standards recommend that firms verify their claims that performance is in compliance with the Standards. If a firm undertakes verification, the verification must be performed by an independent third party. Verification consists of two levels: Level I verification applies to all firm composites; Level II verification applies to specific composites and requires a Level I verification at least on the specific composites being verified at Level II.

When a verification statement is issued, the verifier *must* include in the attestation statement whether a Level I or Level II verification was performed. This statement must be made either in the text of the report or in a footnote. *Without such a statement from the verifier, the firm cannot claim that its investment performance has been verified.*

1. Level I Verification

    This level requires:

    - independent attestation that the requirements of the AIMR-PPS standards have been met on a firmwide basis,
    - that each of the firm's discretionary fee-paying portfolios is included in at least one composite and that the firm's procedures for assigning portfolios to composites are reasonable and have been consistently applied over time, and
    - examination of the firm's procedures for calculating total time-weighted returns, taking into account lost accounts, making appropriate disclosures, and presenting results.

2. Level II Verification

    This level requires that:

    - Level I verification has been performed (at least) on the specific composites being verified at Level II,
    - performance results of specific composites have been calculated according to the AIMR-PPS standards, *and*
    - composites include only appropriate, actual discretionary fee-paying portfolios and do not exclude any other portfolios meeting the same criteria representing a similar strategy or investment objective.

1. Creation and Maintenance of Composites

A composite is an aggregation of a number of portfolios into a single group that is representative of a particular investment strategy, style, or objective. The composite return is the asset-weighted average of the performance results of all the portfolios in the composite. Constructing composites is the first step in implementing the AIMR-PPS standards. Creating meaningful asset-weighted composites is critical to the fair presentation, consistency, and comparability of results over time and among firms.

Requirements

1. General
   a. All actual fee-paying discretionary portfolios must be included in at least one composite defined according to similar strategy or investment objective.
   b. Composites must include new portfolios at the start of the next performance measurement period (at least quarterly) after the portfolio comes under management or according to reasonable and consistently applied firm guidelines.
   c. Composites must exclude terminated portfolios after the last full performance measurement period the portfolios were under management, but composites must continue to include terminated portfolios for all periods prior to termination.
   d. Portfolios must not be switched from one composite to another unless documented changes in client guidelines make switching appropriate.
   e. Convertible and other hybrid securities must be treated consistently across and within composites.
   f. Asset-only returns must not be mixed with asset-plus-cash returns.

2. International

   Subsectors or carve-outs of larger international composites may be used to create stand-alone composites only if the subsectors are actually managed as separate entities with their own cash allocations and currency management.

3. Venture and Private Placements

   All discretionary pooled funds of funds and separately managed portfolios must be included in composites defined by vintage year (i.e., the year of fund formation and first takedown of capital).

Recommendations

1. General

    a. Balanced portfolios should be grouped by allowable range of asset mix.

    b. Accounts with significant cash flows (into or out of portfolios) should treat these cash flows as temporary "new" accounts.

2. International

    For international composites, separate composites should be created for:

    -   portfolios that allow currency hedging (versus those that prohibit currency hedging) unless the use of hedging is judged to be immaterial *and*

    -   portfolios that are managed against hedged benchmarks (versus those that are managed against unhedged benchmarks).

3. Wrap-Fee Accounts

    Wrap-fee portfolios should be grouped in separate composites from nonwrapped composites.

4. Taxable Clients

    a. Portfolios should be grouped by tax rate.

    b. Portfolios may be grouped by vintage year, or similar proxy, to group portfolios with similar amounts of unrealized capital gains.

Composition of Composites

All of a firm's fee-paying discretionary portfolios must be included in one or more appropriate composites. For constructing the composites, the firm must establish reasonable and consistent criteria and must analyze a variety of factors to distinguish and identify the investment strategies, styles, or objectives to be used in grouping the portfolios. Relevant factors include, but are not limited to,

-   investment management styles or strategies,
-   asset classes (e.g., equity, fixed income, real estate, venture capital),
-   risk characteristics of portfolios,
-   the degree of control that the firm has in implementing its investment strategies, and

- characteristics of the clients (e.g., tax status, cash flow needs, risk tolerances).

Once a firm has determined criteria for composite construction, portfolios can be assigned to particular composites.

Questions have arisen about whether a firm can allow offices or branches in different locations (cities, states, regions, and/or countries) to construct their own composites based on their unique or specific portfolios. In some organizations, the location of a branch or office may represent such a unique specific style, strategy, or objective that composites should be constructed based on location. In other organizations, similar styles and investment guidelines are used in multiple locations; composites in these cases should include all similar portfolios of the firm. It is the responsibility of the firm to construct composites in a meaningful, representative manner. In any case, a single branch or office cannot claim compliance with the AIMR-PPS standards for its composites unless either the entire firm is in compliance or the branch/office holds itself out as a separate entity, in which case the single branch is being defined as a firm.

The construction of multiple composites is required if the use of a single composite would be misleading or otherwise inappropriate in the context of the presentation for which the composite results are being used. Thus, for a multiproduct firm, a composite that includes all of the firm's portfolios is unlikely to be meaningful. On the other hand, because the intent of the AIMR-PPS standards is to account for the performance of each portfolio appropriately, a portfolio that represents a unique strategy, style, or objective must be treated as, and must remain, a single-portfolio composite. An aggregation of portfolios with unique investment characteristics into a catch-all, or "junk," composite will not provide meaningful average performance.

Portfolios may not be moved in and out of composites except in the case of valid, documented, client-driven changes in investment objectives or constraints.

Pooled funds, including mutual funds and unit trusts, may be treated as separate composites or combined with other portfolios into one or more composites of the same strategy, style, or objective. Subject to future approval by the U.S. Securities and Exchange Commission (SEC), management fees for such funds may be added back to performance when the fund is combined with separately managed portfolios in a gross-of-fees composite. A firm may use the performance reported by the commingled fund when demonstrating the firm's performance for managing assets invested in the commingled fund. For portfolios invested in more than one pooled fund, the firm must calculate a total return and include the portfolios' performance in a multiple-asset composite.

Discretionary versus Nondiscretionary Portfolios

To claim compliance with the AIMR-PPS standards, all *discretionary* accounts must be included in one or more composites. A portfolio may be considered nondiscretionary only if client-imposed investment restrictions hinder or prohibit the application of the firm's intended investment strategy. Nondiscretionary portfolios must not be included in a firm's discretionary composites.

The AIMR-PPS standards allow the firm to distinguish between discretionary and nondiscretionary portfolios in light of the unique, situational aspects and services of a particular firm. Because no universal definitions of "discretionary" portfolio and "nondiscretionary" portfolio exist, each firm must develop its own definition based on the general principle that a portfolio is nondiscretionary if the portfolio has restrictions that interfere with application of the firm's investment strategy. Examples of restrictions that can render a portfolio nondiscretionary include

- tax considerations that prevent a firm from realizing profit on existing assets and
- client requirements that a portfolio include, or exclude, certain securities or types of securities or include assets that are contrary to the firm's investment strategy.

When particular investments are required to be included in a portfolio or when only limited restrictions are imposed on the portfolio, the firm must determine whether or not the entire portfolio is thereby rendered nondiscretionary. For example, when a firm is directed to include in the portfolio founder's stock, low-cost-basis stock, or investments with sentimental attachments or when the portfolio's management guidelines contain prior-trade approval or other restrictions, the firm could define the entire portfolio as nondiscretionary. Alternatively, a firm could choose to exclude only the nondiscretionary portion of an otherwise discretionary portfolio when constructing composites. The important concept is that the firm apply reasonable, well-documented procedures in a consistent manner when determining whether to include or exclude portfolios with client-imposed investment restrictions.

A firm may provide the performance results of nondiscretionary composites as supplemental information, which can give prospective clients insight into the amount and type of restricted firm assets.

Supplemental information would include such data as percentage of similarly managed institutional assets or percentage of similarly managed private-client assets. Or a firm could create composites of nondiscretionary portfolios based on types of restrictions. For example, all the portfolios that have a significant portion of their assets invested in securities a manager is not free to trade might be included in a composite of portfolios with this common constraint.

The manager determines the bounds of investment discretion, and the manager must follow the bounds consistently. The manager must weight a broad, "inclusive" definition of composite construction against broad dispersion in results. A narrower, "exclusive" definition of composite construction will be revealed through the required disclosures of percentage of firm assets and percentage of taxable assets managed according to the same strategy.

Minimum Portfolio Size

A firm may set size limits to identify portfolios that the firm considers too small to be representative of the firm's intended strategy. These size criteria allow firms to exclude large numbers of portfolios that, in the aggregate, represent a small percentage of total firm assets. Three criteria are allowed for establishing a minimum portfolio size limit:

- Portfolios below the limit are nondiscretionary (i.e., are unable to implement the firm's intended investment strategy).
- Portfolios below the limit represent a small percentage of assets (i.e., are not material).
- The firm does not accept new accounts below the limit.

The AIMR-PPS standards do not specify an allowable percentage for exclusion, but the firm should exclude these portfolios only if doing so has a negligible impact on the firm's asset-weighted average return.

When establishing the criteria for minimum portfolio size for present and past compliance, the firm should consider the criteria applicable for the entire relevant period or periods.

Once a minimum portfolio size has been established, the firm must disclose that information and apply the limit consistently. All discretionary portfolios above the limit must be included in one or more composites.

Terminated Portfolios

Terminated portfolios must be included in an appropriate composite through the last full period they were under firm management.

Survivor-only performance results—that is, those that exclude terminated portfolios—are not in compliance.

Convertibles

Convertibles and other hybrid instruments should be treated consistently among and within composites except when meeting client directives. Convertibles should be treated as equity instruments unless the firm and the client have decided otherwise.

Leverage

Portfolios that use leverage may be included in the same composite with portfolios that do not use leverage as long as the strategies are the same except for leverage. For example, if the strategy involves picking stocks based on fundamental research and the leveraged portfolio simply uses margin always to buy the same stocks in the same relative proportion as the unleveraged portfolio (but totaling more than 100 percent of the account value), then leveraged portfolios and unleveraged portfolios may be included in the same composite, with the adjustment of the total assets of the leveraged portfolio to unleveraged for calculating return.

If the strategy involves any discretion, however, about when and/or how much to leverage (i.e., market timing), then the leverage becomes a separate and distinct strategy and requires separate reporting. In this case, the performance presented must include the effect of the leverage and the firm must present performance on an all-cash basis (which removes the effect of the leverage).

Multiple-Asset Portfolios

Multiple-asset portfolios are portfolios that consist of more than one asset class. Whenever the firm has discretion over changes from one asset class to another, the total return on the entire portfolio must be used in compiling the performance of that portfolio's composite. Therefore, only balanced portfolios for which the firm has discretion over the asset mix are to be included in balanced composites. Balanced portfolios with different asset mixes should be grouped in separate composites defined by the percentages of each asset in the composite portfolios; for example, a balanced portfolio with 60 percent equity and 40 percent bonds would be in a different composite from one with 40 percent equity and 60 percent bonds.

If the firm does not have discretion over the asset mix, the segments of the various asset classes, with their respective cash positions, must be included in composites composed of like assets.

The AIMR-PPS standards do not require that performance of the segments of multiple-asset portfolios be broken out and either presented or included as supplemental information. If the firm wishes to do so, however, the performance of the segments may be displayed in one of two ways:

- as supplemental information to the presentation of the performance of the total multiple-asset portfolio or composite, in which case cash need not be allocated to the segment in calculating returns *or*
- as a stand-alone portfolio (by itself, grouped in a composite with other multiple-asset portfolio segments, or grouped in a composite with single-asset portfolios), in which case cash must be allocated to the segment in calculating the return.

International Portfolios

As in the case of North American portfolios, no absolute rules govern when to include or exclude portfolios of international investments from a composite. Firms are the final judges of which portfolios belong in a composite and which portfolios' restrictions are likely to render the portfolio unrepresentative of a particular style. For example, some firms make country-weighting decisions for their portfolios on the basis of published indexes. For such firms, portfolios managed against different indexes (for instance, one weighted by gross North American product and another weighted by capitalization) belong in separate composites because the country weightings will be different. In contrast, a firm that manages its international portfolios similarly regardless of benchmarks might have only one global composite.

Because portfolios may not be moved in and out of composites except for valid changes in investment objectives or constraints, the decision to include or exclude a multicountry portfolio in a certain composite is important and the implications of all constraints should be considered carefully.

Composites of currency overlay portfolios should be created according to similar benchmarks and restrictions. In currency management, the underlying currency exposure may not matter if portfolios are managed according to similar benchmarks. If the firm is being measured according to the value it adds beyond the existing positions, however, then the underlying currency exposure is critical. In this case, grouping currency overlay portfolios into composites of more than one portfolio would not be meaningful. A series of one-portfolio composites is recommended when composites of multiple-currency overlay portfolios do not provide useful information to prospective clients. The benchmark must parallel the risk or investment style of the composite.

Construction of Composites. The AIMR-PPS standards encourage firms to develop their own objective criteria for constructing composites. Clear and detailed definitions of composites are particularly necessary for multicountry portfolios. Following are examples of guidelines that may be used when constructing composites of international portfolios:

▨ *Portfolios with different benchmarks.* Firms may construct composites on the basis of benchmarks—for example, grouping portfolios measured against the Morgan Stanley Capital International Europe/Australia/Far East (MSCI EAFE) Index separately from portfolios measured against the EAFE Index *ex* Japan.

▨ *Portfolios with different levels of constraints relative to the same benchmark.* Investment restrictions can vary greatly from client to client. A practical and objective way to deal with this problem is to specify a level of constraint on the portfolio for composite membership. For example, a firm could create a composite of portfolios that have global investment objectives and constraints excluding less than 5 percent of the benchmark. This approach would allow inclusion of portfolios that cannot invest in one or two small countries but that, otherwise, the firm believes are representative of the composite's style.

Portfolios that are constrained as to how far their portfolio composition can deviate from the benchmark weightings may not belong in the same composite as portfolios that are completely unconstrained. For example, portfolios that are limited in how far their country weights are allowed to deviate from the index weights might be unrepresentative of a style that can lead to large differences in portfolio country weightings compared with the benchmark weightings.

▨ *Portfolios that invest a large portion of their assets in countries outside the benchmark.* A stated minimum percentage invested in benchmark countries might be useful in defining the composite. For example, a portfolio that invests heavily in emerging markets might be kept in a separate composite from portfolios that invest only in countries included in the EAFE Index.

▨ *Differences in hedging or policies.* If a firm makes significant use of currency hedging when allowed, it should separate portfolios that do not allow such hedging into a different composite and use a different benchmark for the highly hedged and unhedged composites. Similarly, portfolios with materially different risk exposures do not belong in the same composite.

Subsector Composites. Stand-alone composites from subsectors or carve-outs of larger international portfolios can be created only if the subsectors are actually being managed as separate entities with their own cash allocations and currency management—for example, a series of country funds. Results for a subsector that is not being treated as a separate entity may be presented only as supplemental information in presenting the performance of the composite or composites from which the carve-out was drawn.

This requirement for international subsectors is stricter than the subsector requirements for North American portfolios because of

- difficulties in assigning cash to the subsectors of multicurrency portfolios,
- difficulties in assigning results of currency-hedging strategies to subsectors when the hedging strategy was designed for the portfolio as a whole,
- the potential impact of currency-hedging strategies on the subsector's asset allocation (i.e., when the subsector represents an unhedged portion of the portfolio that is not representative of how the subsector would have been managed had currency hedging been allowed), and
- differences in diversification properties for securities held as a small portion of a larger account as compared with securities held in a stand-alone portfolio.

Taxable Portfolios

In the face of the complex issues characteristic of taxable portfolios, in order to form composites, firms must return to the intent of the AIMR-PPS standards: to create a fair and ethical presentation of results.

Many taxable portfolios are subject to unique investment constraints, such as

- the presence of low-cost-basis stock that cannot be sold because of tax repercussions,
- large positions in owner stock that cannot be readily diversified, and

- multiple investment guidelines that may require managing for income rather than for total return.

Such portfolios can be reasonably considered nondiscretionary. For instance, the different tax situations of nuclear-decommissioning trusts, corporate or insurance clients, and private clients may require different investment strategies in terms of emphasizing growth versus yield or dividend versus interest income. If so, firms are required to construct separate composites appropriate to the different strategies.

Even when after-tax performance is adjusted for nondiscretionary capital gains, multiple composites are likely to be required to accommodate client sectors with different tax structures and private clients with different risk tolerances.

Real Estate
Consistent with the general requirements for all composites, all properties with discretionary fee-paying investors must be included in at least one composite. Because of the unique nature of individual real estate investments, however, composites containing single properties are appropriate in many cases.

Venture and Private Placement
The fundamental requirement of the AIMR-PPS standards—the inclusion of all fee-paying portfolios over which the firm has full investment discretion in one or more composites—does not apply to fund raisers. Each alternative investment partnership must be reported separately.

The concept of composites *does* apply to fund-of-funds firms that manage a portfolio of partnerships—using either pooled funds or separately managed accounts. All discretionary investments with the same vintage year must be aggregated into a composite.

For a general partner presenting performance on a venture fund, the partnership's vintage year is determined to be the year in which the fund's initial capital contribution occurred, regardless of the fund formation date. For some buyout funds, however, billing starts before the first drawdown occurs. In this case, the vintage year must be based on the date when funds were first remitted, either for the first takedown or payment of fees.

For a limited partner or investment advisor presenting the performance of separately managed accounts to *existing* clients, the date of the limited partner's initial capital contribution for that client determines the partnership's vintage year. For an investment advisor presenting aggregate performance to *prospective* clients, the date of the first directed capital contribution determines the vintage year. For buyout funds, vintage year must be based on the date when funds were first remitted, either for the first takedown or for the first payment of fees.

After this primary grouping, investments may be aggregated according to similar investment strategies and objectives, and this information may be presented as supplemental. For example, sub-groupings could be constructed on the basis of geography or investment type (venture capital, leveraged buyout, other direct private placement, public securities funds, or venture distribution funds). The common factor required in composite definition is vintage year.

Wrap-Fee Portfolios

The definition of a wrap-fee account (sometimes called an "all-in" account) in the AIMR-PPS standards is the same as the SEC definition of a wrap-fee program. A wrap-fee account is defined by the SEC as

> a program [account] under which any client is charged a specified fee or fees not based directly upon transactions in a client's account for investment advisory services (which may include portfolio management or advice concerning the selection of other investment advisers) and execution of client transactions.

A typical wrap-fee account has a contract or contracts (and fee) involving a broker (sponsor) as the investment advisor, other services (custody, consulting, reporting, performance, selection, monitoring, and execution of trades), and the client (brokerage customer). It is an all-inclusive, asset-based brokerage relationship, which may include other services; it is not a trust account, mutual fund, typical brokerage account, or private investment advisory relationship.

Differing portfolio fee structures may be a factor in composite construction but should not be the determining criterion for a portfolio's inclusion or exclusion in an otherwise representative composite. Nevertheless, the AIMR-PPS standards recommend that wrap-fee accounts be grouped in separate composites from non-wrapped composites because transaction fees (required to be netted by the AIMR-PPS standards) and advisory fees (not required to be netted) cannot be segregated uniformly by accounts and firms in a wrap-fee situation.

2. Calculation of Returns

Achieving comparability among investment management firms' performance requires uniformity in methods used to calculate returns. The AIMR-PPS standards allow flexibility in performance calculation. However, performance must be calculated using a methodology that incorporates the time-weighted total rate of return concept. Firms may use alternative performance calculations for portfolios and composites so long as the calculation method chosen represents performance fairly, is not misleading, and is applied consistently to all portfolios and time periods.

Requirements

1. General

    a. Total return, including realized and unrealized gains plus income, must be used when calculating investment performance.

    b. Time-weighted rates of return must be used.

    c. Accrual accounting must be used for fixed-income and all other securities that accrue income. Accrued income must be included in the market value calculation of the denominator and the numerator.

    d. Composites must be asset weighted using beginning-of-period weightings.

    e. Returns from cash and cash equivalents held in portfolios must be included in return calculations, and the cash and cash equivalents must be included in the portfolio amount (total assets) on which the return is calculated.

    f. Portfolios must be valued at least quarterly, and periodic returns must be geometrically linked.

    g. Performance must be calculated after the deduction of trading expenses (e.g., broker commissions and SEC fees), if any.

    h. When portfolios use leverage to purchase securities, return results must be calculated on both an actual basis and a restated, "all cash" basis. For a composite that consists of externally leveraged and unleveraged accounts (for example, securities on margin), the leveraged accounts must be restated to all cash when the return of the composite is computed.

    i. All documents must be maintained that are necessary to form the basis for or demonstrate the calculation of the performance or rate of return of all managed accounts that the advisor includes in a composite (current and historical performance results).

2. International

The benchmark for any currency overlay portfolio must be calculated in accordance with the mandate of the portfolio unless the benchmark is actually the currency return on a published benchmark.

3. Taxable Clients

For after-tax composites:

    a. Taxes must be recognized in the same period as when the taxable event occurred.

    b. Taxes on income and realized capital gains must be subtracted from results regardless of whether taxes are paid from assets outside the account or from account assets.

    c. The maximum federal income tax rates appropriate to the portfolios must be assumed.

    d. The return for after-tax composites that hold both taxable and tax-exempt securities must be adjusted to an after-tax basis rather than being "grossed up" to a taxable equivalent.

    e. Calculation of after-tax returns for tax-exempt bonds must include amortization and accretion of premiums or discounts.

    f. Taxes on income are to be recognized on an accrual basis.

4. Real Estate

    a. Real estate must be valued through an independent appraisal at least once every three years unless client agreements state otherwise.

    b. Real estate valuations must be reviewed at least quarterly.

    c. Component returns for participating or convertible mortgages must be allocated as follows:

- basic cash interest to income return,
- contingent interest (current receivable) to income return,
- basic accrued interest (deferred) to income return,
- additional contingent interest (deferred; payable at ma-

turity, prepayment, or sale) to appreciation return,

- return that is currently payable from operations to income return, and
- all other sources of income that are deferred or realizable in the future to the appreciation component.

5. Venture and Private Placements
   a. General partners
      - Cumulative internal rate of return (IRR) must be presented since inception of the fund and be net of fees, expenses, and carry to the limited partner.
      - IRR must be calculated based on cash-on-cash returns plus residual value.
   b. Intermediaries and investment advisors
      - For separately managed accounts and commingled fund-of-funds structures, cumulative IRR must be presented since inception of the fund and be net of fees, expenses, and carry to the limited partners but gross of investment advisory fees unless net of fees is required to meet applicable regulatory requirements.
      - Calculation of IRR must be based on an aggregation of all the appropriate partnership cash flows into one IRR calculation—as if from one investment.

Recommendations

1. General
   a. Equal-weighted composites should be calculated in addition to, but not instead of, asset-weighted composites.
   b. Accrual accounting for dividends (as of the ex-dividend date) is recommended.
   c. Accrual accounting for fixed-income securities, although required only after the applicable implementation date, is strongly recommended for *all* performance periods.
   d. Accrued interest should be included in market value calculations in both the numerator *and* denominator for all periods, although the inclusion is required only after the applicable implementation date.
   e. Portfolios should be valued on a daily basis or, if not daily,

whenever cash flows and market action combine to materially distort performance.

f. Trade-date accounting should be used.

2. International

a. A consistent source of exchange rates should be used.

b. Returns should be calculated net of withholding taxes on dividends, interest, and capital gains.

c. Whenever the currency overlay manager is notified of changes in the underlying currency exposures as a result of a shift in the underlying assets, the currency overlay portfolios should be revalued (e.g., for attribution purposes).

3. Taxable Clients

a. Cash-basis accounting is to be used if required by applicable law.

b. Calculations should be adjusted for nondiscretionary capital gains.

c. Benchmark returns should be calculated using the actual turnover in the benchmark index, if available; otherwise, an approximation is acceptable.

d. If returns are presented before taxes, a total rate of return for the composite should be presented without adjustment for tax-exempt income to a pretax basis.

4. Real Estate

Income earned at the investment level should be included in the computation of income return regardless of the investor's accounting policies for recognizing income from real estate investments.

5. Venture and Private Placement

a. General partners

• Standard industry guidelines should be used for valuation of venture capital investments,

• valuation should be either cost or discount to comparables in the public market for buyout, mezzanine, distressed, or special situation investments, and

• IRR should be calculated net of fees, expenses, and carry without public stocks discounted and assuming stock distributions were held.

  b. Net cumulative IRR (after deduction of advisory fees and any other administrative expenses or carried interest) should be calculated for separately managed accounts, managed accounts, and commingled fund-of-funds structures.

Calculation of Performance

The performance of portfolios must be reported using the time-weighted total rate of return. The AIMR-PPS standards do not require revision of existing performance calculations or associated computer software that conform to the concepts of quarterly time-weighted total returns. Rather, for those who desire a single guide-line, this section contains widely used definitions, formulas, and methodologies for each kind of calculation.[1]

Total Return

The calculation of total return in the absence of cash flows for a period (i.e., a month or quarter) is based on the formula

$$R_{TR} = \frac{MVE - MVB}{MVB},$$

where R_{TR} is the total return (sometimes referred to as the "non-weighted rate of return"), MVE is the market value of the portfolio at the end of the period, including all income accrued up to the end of the period, and MVB is the portfolio's market value at the begin-ning of the period, including all income accrued up to the end of the previous period.

  This well-known formula represents growth (or decline) in the value of a portfolio, including both capital appreciation and income, as a proportion of the starting market value. This unweighted rate of return is a reasonable way of presenting the performance of a portfolio with no cash flows over a period. The condition of no cash flows is frequently violated, however, in the normal management of a client's account. Cash flows *do* occur, often unpredictably.

  If cash flows occur during the period, theoretically, they must be used to "buy" additional units of the portfolio at the market price on the day they are received. Thus, the most accurate method of calculating return is to calculate the market value of the portfolio on

-----

[1]The reader should recognize that arithmetic notations vary among outside texts and reference materials.

the date of each cash flow, calculate an interim rate of return for the subperiod according to the preceding formula, and then link the subperiod returns to get the return for the month or quarter. This approach removes the effect of each cash flow. Methods that use this approach, or an approximation of it, are called *time-weighted rate-of-return* methods.

Time-Weighted Rate of Return. The AIMR-PPS standards require calculation of a time-weighted rate of return using a minimum of quarterly valuations and geometric linking of these interim returns. Approximation methods are acceptable.

This section describes three methods to compute time-weighted rate of return. The first is the daily valuation method (or valuation whenever cash flows occur), which is considered the ideal and, therefore, preferred. Two other methods—the modified Dietz method and the modified Bank Administration Institute (BAI) method—result in approximations of the daily valuation method.

▨ *Daily valuation method.* The formula for valuing the portfolio whenever cash flows occur is

$$R_{DAILY} = (S_1 \times S_2 \times \ldots S_n) - 1,$$

where S_1, S_2, . . ., S_n are the subperiod indexes for subperiods 1, 2, etc., through n.

Note that calculating R_{DAILY} does not require determining the subperiod returns. If desired, the subperiod return, R_i, can be determined from the subperiod index by the formula

$$R_i = S_i - 1.$$

Subperiod 1 extends from the first day of the period up to and including the date of the first cash flow. Subperiod 2 begins the next day and extends to the date of the second cash flow, and so forth. The final subperiod extends from the day after the final cash flow through the last day of the period.

Each of the subperiod indexes is calculated using the formula

$$S_i = \frac{MVE_i}{MVB_i},$$

where MVE_i is the market value of the portfolio at the end of subperiod i, before any cash flows in period i but including accrued income for the period, and MVB_i is the market value at the end of the previous subperiod (i.e., the beginning of this subperiod), including any cash flows at the end of the previous subperiod and including accrued income up to the end of the previous period.

The chief advantage of this method is that it calculates the true time-weighted rate of return rather than an estimate. The major drawback is that it requires precise valuation of the portfolio on the date of each cash flow, something that is not always feasible or practical. Also, if all securities are not accurately priced for each subperiod valuation, errors generated in the return calculation using the daily valuation method may be greater than the errors caused by using the approximation methods. In such cases, it is important to be able to back out and correct for errors, such as missed security splits, mispricings, and improperly booked transactions, because day-to-day compounding will not always correct for them automatically.

 Modified Dietz method. The Dietz method overcomes the need to know the valuation of the portfolio on the date of each cash flow by assuming a constant rate of return on the portfolio during the period. The original Dietz method assumed that all cash flows occurred at the midpoint of the period. The modified Dietz method weights each cash flow by the amount of time it is held in the portfolio. The formula for estimating the time-weighted rate of return using the modified Dietz method is

$$R_{DIETZ} = \frac{MVE - MVB - F}{MVB + FW},$$

where MVE and MVB are as defined previously, F is the sum of the cash flows within the period (contributions to the portfolio are positive flows, and withdrawals or distributions are negative flows), and FW is the sum of each cash flow, F_i, multiplied by its weight, W_i.

Weight W_i is the proportion of the total number of days in the period that cash flow F_i has been in (or out of) the portfolio. The formula for W_i is

$$W_i = \frac{CD - D_i}{CD},$$

where CD is the total number of days in the period and D_i is the number of days since the beginning of the period in which cash flow F_i occurred.

The numerator is based on the assumption that the cash flows occur at the end of the day. If cash flows were assumed to occur at the beginning of the day, the numerator would be $CD + 1 - D_i$. Whichever method is chosen, being consistent is important.

The chief advantage of the modified Dietz method is that it does not require portfolio valuation for the date of each cash flow. Its chief disadvantage is that it provides a less accurate estimate of the true time-weighted rate of return. The estimate suffers most when a combination of the following conditions exists: (1) one or more large cash flows occurred; (2) cash flows occur during periods of high market volatility—that is, the portfolio's returns have been significantly nonlinear.

▨ *Modified BAI method.* The modified BAI method determines the internal rate of return for the period. Like the original Dietz method, the original BAI method has been modified to take into effect the exact timing of each cash flow. In the BAI approach, the IRR is that value of R that satisfies the following equation:

$$MVE = \sum F_i (1 + R)^{W_i},$$

where MVE and W_i are the same as for the modified Dietz method. The cash flows, F_i, are also the same as with the Dietz method with one important exception: The market value at the start of the period is also treated as a cash flow; that is, $MVB = F_0$.

The IRR is obtained by selecting values for R and solving the equation until the result equals MVE. For example, if three cash flows (including the market value at the start of the period) have occurred, the computational formula will have three terms:

$$MV_{END} = F_0 (1 + R)^{W_0} + F_1 (1 + R)^{W_1} + F_2 (1 + R)^{W_2}.$$

The first term deals with the first cash flow, F_0, which is the value of the portfolio at the beginning of the period; W_i is the proportion of the period that the cash flow F_i was in (or out of) the portfolio. Because F_0 is in for the whole period, $W_0 = 1$. The larger the value of F_i in the term, the more it will contribute to the total, but the smaller the exponent (i.e., the value of W_i), the less the term will contribute to the sum. The usual effect is that the first term, with a large F_0 and W_0 equal to 1, will contribute far more than the other terms.

The advantages and disadvantages of the modified BAI method are the same as those of the modified Dietz method. The modified BAI method has the additional disadvantage of requiring an iterative process solution and is thus less desirable than the Dietz when manual calculation is required. Calculator and computer programs are available, however, for solving IRR.

Note that the modified Dietz method is identical to the first-order approximation of the modified BAI method. For most purposes, the second-order approximation of the modified BAI method provides sufficiently accurate results. The selection of methodology should be based on which methodology will most accurately convey the portfolios' investment style and can be used practically.

Income. The AIMR-PPS standards require that interest income be calculated on an accrual basis.

The guiding principle in determining what income to report is as follows: Include the income that would have been received had the security actually been sold at the end of the performance period. For example, most fixed-income securities accrue income on a pro rata basis. This income is payable at the coupon date or when the security is sold, so it must be accrued unless the price of the security already reflects such accrual. Dividends are not payable unless the stock was owned on the ex-dividend date. Therefore, dividends should be accrued as income on the ex-dividend date for trade valuations (note that this approach is a recommendation, not a requirement; cash-basis accounting for equities is acceptable if it does not distort performance).

Questions have arisen about whether income on cash and cash equivalents should be accounted for on an accrual or cash basis and whether these positions should be considered fixed-income securities. An investment management firm may determine how to categorize cash instruments based on the strategy associated with the instruments' inclusion in a portfolio. For example, one firm may be using U.S. T-bills to implement a fixed-income strategy whereas another firm is holding the T-bills as a cash substitute. If a cash instrument is categorized as a fixed-income instrument, then accrual accounting is required. In either case, some form of accrual accounting should be used for interest—either based on the prior periodic interest rate (e.g., for a STIF [short-term investment fund]account) or based on a weighted average of the actual periodic short-term interest rates. Estimates by either method should be adjusted in the following period to reflect actual interest earned.

Interest income must be included in the beginning and ending portfolio market values or be accounted for when performance is calculated. Interest should be accrued for a security in the portfolio using whatever method is customary and appropriate for that security. The most frequent method of accruing interest on a U.S. fixed-income security, other than U.S. Treasury issues, is the 30/360-day count method. This method assumes that each month has 30 days, and it assumes a 360-day year. Accounts using differing time periods would use a different calculation method.

Using the 30/360-day count method, the formula for calculating the number of days over which interest has accrued is

$$360(Y_2 - Y_1) + 30(M_2 - M_1) + (D_2 - D_1),$$

where Y_1, M_1, and D_1 are, respectively, the year, month, and day of the previous coupon date and Y_2, M_2, and D_2 are, respectively, the year, month, and day of the settlement date. In calculating accrued interest over a performance period, Y_2, M_2, and D_2 can refer to the end-of-period date and Y_1, M_1, and D_1 to the end-of-period date of the previous period.

Some U.S. Treasury discount instruments and zero-coupon bonds already include accrued income as part of their market prices. If income for these instruments is being accrued as part of the income process, it should be deducted from the market price to avoid counting the accrued income twice. That is, market price should be divided into two amounts—the principal amount and the accrued interest.

Income earned by a fund with stable net asset value, commonly called a money market or short-term investment fund, may be estimated on the basis of the previous period, accrued at that rate, and adjusted at the end of the period by using cash-basis accounting.

Calculating Composite Performance

A composite is an aggregation of individual portfolios or asset classes representing similar investment objectives or strategies. The composite return is intended to be a single value that reflects the overall performance (the "central tendency") of the set. The objective in reporting the returns of composites is to use a method for reporting the composite return that will give the same value as if the composite were treated as one "master portfolio." That is, the calculated value is the same value that would result if all of the assets and transactions of the individual portfolios/classes were combined and the return were computed using the procedures discussed in this chapter.

Equal-Weighted Return (Simple Average). Simply averaging the performance of all the portfolios in a composite, regardless of size, will provide an equal-weighted composite return. This simple method will provide an accurate "master portfolio" return, however, only in the unlikely event that the market values of all portfolios are exactly the same or all the portfolio returns are identical. The simple average, together with the standard deviation, does provide a measure of the ability of a manager to obtain consistent returns for all portfolios regardless of size.

Asset-Weighted Return (Market-Value-Weighted Average). The AIMR-PPS standards are based on the principle of asset-weighted returns. If a composite contains two portfolios, one of which is 10 times the size of the other, the rate of return for the larger portfolio should have more impact on the composite return than that of the smaller portfolio. The asset-weighted return method accomplishes this by weighting the contributions to the composite rate of return by the beginning market values of its constituent portfolios. This method will give the same value as if the composite were treated as one master portfolio.

Asset-Weighted and Cash-Flow-Weighted Return. The asset-weighted and cash-flow-weighted method represents a refinement to the asset-weighted approach. Consider the case in which one of two portfolios in a composite doubles in market value as the result of a contribution on the first day of a performance period. Under the asset-weighted approach, this portfolio will be weighted in the composite based solely on its beginning market value (i.e., not including the contribution). The asset-weighted and cash-flow-weighted method resolves this problem by including the effect of cash flows in the weighting calculation as well as in the market values.

Aggregate Return. This method combines the composite assets and cash flows to calculate performance as if the composite were one portfolio. The method is also acceptable as an asset-weighted approach.

Examples of Calculating Composite Performance. The AIMR-PPS standards require asset weighting of the portfolio returns within a composite using one of the methods discussed: beginning-of-period weightings, beginning-of-period market values plus weighted cash flows, or aggregating assets and cash flows to calculate performance as for a single portfolio. The choice of methodology for calculating returns should reflect investment policies, where applicable. In some cases, such as where the investments are not adjusted for new cash flows intraperiod or cash flows are infrequent and proportionally insignificant, the use of one methodology as opposed to another may provide a more accurate return for the composite.

The AIMR-PPS standards recommend that equal-weighted returns be reported as supplemental information. The equal-weighted return is the simple (unweighted) mean of the individual portfolio returns. The formula for the equal-weighted composite return, C_{EQUAL}, is

$$C_{EQUAL} = \frac{R_1 + R_2 + \ldots R_n}{n},$$

where R_1 is the return for the first portfolio in the composite and n is the number of portfolios in the composite.

The asset-weighted composite return, C_{ASSET}, may be calculated by the formula

$$C_{ASSET} = \frac{\sum (MVB_i \times R_i)}{MVB_{TOTAL}},$$

where MVB_1 is the beginning market value (at the start of the period) for a portfolio, R_i is the rate of return for portfolio i, and MVB_{TOTAL} is the total market value at the beginning of the period for all the portfolios in the composite. (Note that, in accordance with AIMR PPS standards on composite construction, no portfolios added or terminated during the period should be included in this calculation.)

The composite returns must be calculated at least quarterly (monthly is preferred). If monthly composite returns are calculated, the monthly returns are linked geometrically using this formula:

$$C_{QT} = (1 + C_{MO1})(1 + C_{MO2})(1 + C_{MO3}) - 1,$$

where C_{QT} is the composite quarterly return and C_{MO1}, C_{MO2}, and C_{MO3} are the composite returns for months 1, 2, and 3, respectively.

Similarly, to compute the annual rate of return for composite returns calculated quarterly, the formula to use is

$$C_Y = (1 + C_{Q1})(1 + C_{Q2})(1 + C_{Q3})(1 + C_{Q4}) - 1,$$

where C_{Q1}, C_{Q2}, C_{Q3}, and C_{Q4} are composite returns for Quarters 1, 2, 3, and 4, respectively.

Valuation Periods and Weighting
The pricing of all assets must be based on a reasonable estimate of the current value of assets if they were sold on that date to a willing buyer. In cases of frequently traded securities, standardized pricing

quotations must be used and must be supportable. In the case of thinly traded securities, the firm may use any reasonable method for valuation as long as the method is consistently applied. Amortization or accretion valuation methods for cash and cash-equivalent positions are permitted as long as that valuation method reasonably approximates market value.

The AIMR-PPS standards recommend that a portfolio be revalued when cash flows and market action combine to cause a material distortion of performance. A material distortion is deemed to occur when cash flows exceed 10 percent of the portfolio's market value. Daily valuations are encouraged because distortions in performance from cash flows decrease when portfolios are valued frequently.

The AIMR-PPS standards require that beginning-of-period market values be used to weight the portfolio returns in a composite. Beginning-of-period values represent the desired "master portfolio" result better than do end-of-period values.

In computing the quarterly composite return, each portfolio's return is weighted by the beginning-of-quarter market value for the portfolio. If portfolios are valued monthly and linked to get the quarterly return, the return is calculated using the size-weighted composite return for each month and these monthly returns are linked to get the quarterly return.

An even more precise value can be obtained by using the asset-weighted and cash-flow-weighted method.

Allocating Cash

Performance results for any portfolio must include cash, cash equivalents, and substitute assets. Cash allocation must be made at the beginning of the reporting period, and cash must be allocated in a way that is representative of the intended style. Acceptable methods

- must allow for an *ex ante* (beginning-of-period) decision to allocate cash,
- must meet the tests of being reasonable and representative, and
- should allow for an audit trail that provides evidence of the cash allocation decision.

The characteristics of the *ex ante* decision making and the audit trail must be replicated for retroactive cash allocation. Unless a manager can identify a method that accurately represents what the historical cash allocation would have been, retroactive cash allocation should not be attempted.

The AIMR-PPS standards require that cash be allocated to the segment returns of a multiple-asset portfolio when segment returns are being presented either alone or as part of a single-asset composite as evidence of the firm's ability to manage the segment by itself. This cash allocation to each of the segments must be made at the beginning of each reporting period. The rest of this section discusses the several different methods of cash allocation that are acceptable.

Separate Portfolios. This approach splits the multiple-asset funds into separate portfolios based on asset class. The portfolios may be merged for client reporting and may be measured separately for performance purposes. This method is conceptually simple and is available on some portfolio management systems with no modifications. A disadvantage is that separate portfolios increase the work load involved in portfolio administration by increasing the number of portfolios that must be managed. The approach also complicates money market management by increasing the number of portfolios that must be traded.

Multiple Cash Balances. This approach involves maintaining separate cash balances for the segments within a single multiple-asset portfolio. This method thus retains the original number of portfolios. The effort involved in administration differs little, however, from the separate portfolios approach. Short-term trading must still be segregated by asset class, and cash transactions have to be entered to move cash from one segment to another. Managers must maintain a decision matrix to direct which cash balance will be affected by each of the various transaction types. Problems of interpretation can also arise in international trading, when, for example, a German asset is settled in U.S. dollars.

Allocation of Cash Returns. This approach involves the allocation of rates of return rather than the maintenance of actual separate cash balances. In this approach, cash and equivalents are maintained as a single entity in the multiple-asset portfolio. The rate of return is determined for cash and equivalents and for all the asset segments. The cash and cash-equivalent returns are then allocated to the segment returns to create segment-plus-cash returns. This approach has a minimal impact on current management and administration practices. It does not require segregating short-term trading by asset class, increasing the number of portfolios, or developing a decision matrix for the cash effects of trading.

Determination of the appropriate method for allocating cash returns is the responsibility of the investment firm, but once the method is established, the firm must apply it consistently. Many acceptable ways of allocating cash returns can be imagined; the following two methods are examples of acceptable approaches.

▧ *Predetermined cash allocation mix applied to residual cash.* At the beginning of the reporting period, the firm sets a cash allocation mix (e.g., 60 percent stocks, 40 percent bonds) and allocates residual cash accordingly. This approach is appropriate for strategies that call for nearly 100 percent investment at all times; in such cases, the effect of residual cash has a minimal impact on the single-asset results when this approach is used.

▧ *Cash allocation based on target asset-class percentages determined at the beginning of the period.* Actual asset allocations are compared with the beginning-of-period target allocations. If a segment is underinvested relative to its beginning-of-period target, the differential is drawn from residual cash plus cash equivalents, and the appropriate cash return is applied.

If a segment is overinvested relative to its beginning-of-period target, the segment borrows from cash and cash equivalents; the borrowing cost is the cash segment return (cash and cash equivalents). This borrowing cost is deducted from the single-asset return. This approach allows the possibility of a negative cash balance; it might also imply that the investment strategy uses leverage.

Also, actual asset allocations may be compared with the beginning-of-period target allocations if the return weights are adjusted by purchases, sales, contributions, withdrawals, and income. In this approach, the target allocations are readjusted to reflect active allocation decisions by the manager throughout the period.

Finally, borrowing may also occur between segments other than the cash segment. If an asset segment is underinvested, assets are allocated to meet the beginning-of-period target. If residual cash is insufficient, however, borrowing occurs between the other segments. In this case, instead of using a blended return of segment plus cash and cash equivalents, therefore, the manager applies blended returns based on segment returns. Overweighted segments borrow at a segment cost, and underinvested segments are mixed with segment returns rather than with the cash return.

Trading Expenses

Performance is to be calculated after the deduction of trading and other expenses that the firm controls (e.g., commissions, SEC fees). Custodial fees are not charged against performance. The treatment of a brokerage firm's annual charges as a cash withdrawal rather than as a charge against performance will depend on whether this annual fee is in lieu of separately levied transaction costs. For example, if this fee is really a commission, then it should be deducted from performance. If it is a custodial fee, it should not be charged against performance and should be treated as a cash flow withdrawal.

Leverage

Return results must be calculated on a basis that includes the effect of leverage. Furthermore, return results must be restated to an all-cash basis when the portfolio used leverage and the same securities could have been purchased at the same prices if the portfolio had the cash to do so. Results should be restated to an all-cash basis only when the necessary restatement can be based entirely on actual transactions and can be verified in accordance with applicable account standards, including third-party documentation (such as client agreements about asset allocation or client guidelines on portfolio strategies and objectives).

The all-cash return must be computed and, in all cases, used or disclosed—either as required supplemental information when the leverage is at the manager's discretion or as the only reported return when the leverage is mandated by the client and thus nondiscretionary. The principle that requires the all-cash restatement is that buying stocks is possible on an all-cash basis; therefore, the portfolio could have bought the same stocks at the same prices if it had actually had the cash to do so.

The computation of the all-cash return, R_{AC}, is as follows:

$$R_{AC} = \frac{MVE + \text{Interest}_{MARGIN}}{MVB},$$

where MVE is the total market value of the assets at the end of the period, MVB is the total market value of the assets at the beginning of the period, including the margin borrowing, and Interest_{MARGIN} is the expense of margin interest during the period. The margin interest is added back to the total asset value because, under the assumption of all cash, the portfolio would not have incurred the expense of borrowing.

It is not permissible to assume a certain cash rate of return for assets committed to but not yet received by the firm. For example, a client might commit to investing $100 million but put up only $20 million and the firm might then make a forward commitment for the full $100 million. As the money comes in, it goes to cash. In this instance, the firm cannot add an assumed interest rate to the $80 million cash balance outstanding. The firm could disclose that returns might be conservative because the firm engages in forward contracts to protect the client from price volatility and does not earn interest on the full cash amount until received.

The incremental return from derivative securities is equal to the difference between the total fund return and the return on the fund without the contribution of the derivative securities. The incremental return should be calculated whenever (1) such a calculation is representative of the true incremental return attributable to derivatives and (2) the necessary calculation is based entirely on actual transactions or on third-party documentation that can be used to verify the calculation. Causes of nonrepresentative calculations include, but are not limited to, the use of derivatives affecting the execution of the portfolio strategy in the remainder of the fund or affecting prices of transactions in the remainder of the fund.

Any change in margin debt during the period must be treated as cash flow to the total assets because such a change in margin debt occurs concurrently with an identical change in total assets. All other requirements and guidelines related to calculating time-weighted total returns, revaluation of the portfolio for cash flows, and so on, must be applied.

Trade-Date Accounting

Trade-date accounting is recommended when calculating performance, although settlement-date accounting is acceptable if disclosed. Because of the volatility and lengthy settlement periods of some markets, trade-date accounting is strongly recommended for calculating the performance of international portfolios.

Calculating Returns for International Assets

Conversion of the benchmark and the portfolio into the base currency should be carried out using the same exchange rates, if possible. If this is not possible, the firm should disclose any significant deviations. An example of a situation in which the same exchange rates cannot be used is the case in which the market and/or points in time used for pricing currencies in the benchmark and in the composite portfolios are different.

"Base currency" refers to the currency of the country in which the investor is based. For example, for a U.S-based investor, the base currency would be the U.S. dollar. "Local currency" refers to the currency of the country of interest. For example, yen would be the local currency for the Japanese component of a portfolio. Firms may choose which exchange rates to use to convert performance. A method should be determined and consistently applied.

Currency Overlay Portfolios. This section defines the four broad categories of currency overlay portfolios and discusses the calculation of returns for such portfolios:

- Portfolios whose objectives are to add value and/or control risk relative to the unhedged (by the overlay manager) portfolio. The objective of this strategy might be to achieve a positive gain from hedging relative to zero or, alternatively, to achieve a total currency return (combining the returns from the currency exposure of the underlying assets with the returns from hedging) in excess of zero.
- Portfolios for which the benchmark is the underlying assets of the portfolio hedged back to a base currency in some proportion. The benchmarks of portfolios in this category have a predetermined fixed-percentage exposure in the base currency; for example, a "50 percent hedged into U.S. dollars" benchmark has an overall dollar exposure of 50 percent. If the underlying portfolio already has U.S. dollars—via exposure to the U.S. equity market, for example—then the possibility is that no hedging will be required to calculate the benchmark because the dollar exposure may already be 50 percent. In this case, the firm may even need to "sell" some dollars to calculate the benchmark. If the benchmark does require further hedging to achieve its 50 percent dollar exposure, however, the benchmark is calculated in such a way that the same proportion of each currency is sold.
- Portfolios with asset-based benchmarks. These situations are similar to the previous category, but for the same "50 percent hedged into U.S. dollars" example, 50 percent of all nondollar currencies would be sold into U.S. dollars regardless of the U.S. dollar exposure already inherent in the underlying assets. So, the benchmark might well have a U.S. dollar exposure greater than 50 percent.
- Portfolios whose benchmarks are published, either specifically for a portfolio or generally. An example is the currency return of the MSCI EAFE Index 100 percent hedged into U.S. dollars.

In accordance with the AIMR-PPS standards, currency overlay portfolios must be valued at least quarterly, but because of the volatile nature of these portfolios, firms may need to revalue currency overlay portfolios more frequently than quarterly to obtain full and fair disclosure. In addition, returns on currency overlay portfolios should be recalculated whenever the overlay manager receives notification of a change in the underlying assets (e.g., revaluation of assets from the custodian).

Two portfolios with the same benchmark may give different mandates to the overlay portfolio managers. For example, when the mandate is based on the underlying assets, the return of the overlay performance benchmark will be different unless the underlying assets of two portfolios imply identical currency exposures. Consequently, the performance benchmark for any currency overlay portfolio must be calculated in accordance with the mandate of the portfolio (unless the benchmark is actually the currency return on a published benchmark).

Total returns of the composite and the benchmark must be shown on the same basis. Each composite's return should be accompanied by any relevant information regarding restrictions—such as a target benchmark, no cross hedging, no net short positions, and so on.

Benchmark Reporting: Gross versus Net of Withholding Taxes. Foreign taxes that may be recoverable on financial transactions by a foreign investor, depending on tax status and national treaties, present a performance problem unique to international investors. The AIMR-PPS standards recommend calculation of portfolio returns net of withholding taxes on dividends, interest, and capital gains. Some comparison benchmarks are published on a "gross" and on a "net" basis. In these benchmarks, "gross" refers to a total return that includes capital appreciation plus income and makes no reduction for withholding taxes and "net" refers to a gross return that includes interest or dividend income but is "net of withholding taxes." Firms must disclose whether composite and benchmark returns are net of foreign withholding taxes and must disclose the assumed withholding tax rate used to calculate a benchmark net total return. Computation of a benchmark return as net of withholding taxes will be easier and provide a more appropriate bogey to be measured against.

The effects of withholding taxes on equity returns will depend on the investor's base country. The United States has tax treaties with many countries under which U.S. investors receive tax credits from the U.S. government for taxes paid in the foreign country. Tax-exempt investors frequently receive withheld tax from foreign governments, and no U.S. withholding tax is levied against U.S.-based pension funds.

Ideally, calculation of net index returns should be from the tax perspective of the client. Calculation of net index returns from each perspective could be complex, however, because of data limitations. The MSCI net dividend indexes, among the most widely used, assume a worst-case tax perspective—that of a Luxembourg holding company. Luxembourg has few tax treaties, and Luxembourg-based investors pay the maximum of dividend taxes. Over the 23 years ending on December 31, 1992, the MSCI Luxembourg-based EAFE Index, on a gross total return basis, rose an annualized 12.65 percent as compared with return on a net basis in U.S. dollar terms of 11.72 percent.

A widely used methodology for calculating monthly net-of-dividend-tax benchmarks is

$$\left\{ \frac{\text{Current price index}}{\text{Previous price index}} \left[\left(\frac{\text{Current monthly yield}}{100} \right) (1 - \text{Withholding tax\%}) + 1 \right] - 1 \right\} \times 100.$$

Exhibit 1 provides an illustration of this calculation.

Exhibit 1. Return to Australian Portfolio in U.S. Dollars

Current price index	201.466
Previous price index	210.936
Annualized yield	4.2
Monthly yield	0.35
Withholding tax	30%
Published returns (%)	
Price	–4.49
Net	–4.25

Calculation:

$$\left(\frac{201.466}{210.936} \left[\frac{0.35}{100} (1 - 0.30) + 1 \right] - 1 \right) \times 100 = -4.25\%.$$

The handling of income in some international indexes (e.g., the Financial Times and MSCI indexes) is imprecise because income is applied monthly as 1/12 the annual dividend yield rather than dividends being accounted for as they are received.

Some fixed-income portfolio benchmarks are calculated net of withholding taxes. As with equity portfolios, the actual impact of taxes depends on the investor's home country. For example, U.S.-based investors are subject to a 10 percent withholding tax in Japan, whereas Japan-based investors are not subject to that tax. The same "net" benchmark could thus not be used for both investors. Currently, Salomon Brothers offers its aggregate and component global bond indexes net of taxes from the perspective of a U.S.-based pension plan.

Tax Calculations

For calculating after-tax results of current clients' portfolios, taxes on income and realized capital gains must be subtracted from the results or from composite results whether taxes are paid from assets outside the account or from account assets. Likewise, the firm must be given credit for the potential tax advantages of realizing losses.

The tax rates assumed for an after-tax composite must be the maximum federal tax rates appropriate to that type of client for each year. State and local taxes should not be deducted in calculations for composites. Reporting of after-tax results to current clients may be based on actual tax rates with or without state and local taxes.

Taxes should be recognized in the same period as when the taxable event occurred. For example, if a capital gain is taken in November of Year 1 but the tax is not paid until April of Year 2, the after-tax performance should be reduced in the fourth quarter of Year 1 by the amount of taxes to be incurred.

The treatment of taxes on income is more complex than the treatment of taxes on capital gains. The AIMR-PPS standards require accrual accounting for income on fixed-income securities. To remain consistent with the general AIMR-PPS standards, and to mitigate the distortions that could occur (with bonds that pay income once yearly, for example), taxes on income from fixed-income securities are to be recognized on an accrual basis. When actual taxes are not paid for several months, this approach is conservative.

A major difficulty in reporting after-tax performance in a manner that is fair to the investment firm is the need to adjust the return for capital gains taxes that were sustained because of client withdrawals. When after-tax returns are presented for the purpose of comparing after-tax results of different portfolios or composites, the calculation should include an adjustment for such nondiscretionary capital gains. This calculation is used to provide comparability among manager after-tax returns, which are different from clients' actual returns, or economic returns (see Appendix B definition).

One method that would enable firms to adjust their after-tax returns for the realization of capital gains would be to flag each transaction to indicate that realization was either firm directed or client directed. In the calculation of after-tax performance, the firm would reflect only those taxes on capital gains from firm-directed transactions. Such flagging would necessitate a major (and probably expensive) change, however, in accounting software.

A simpler approach would be to make the (admittedly, imperfect) assumption that if a firm is required to sell assets to meet a client withdrawal, the capital gains will have to be realized, on average, in the same proportion that such gains exist in the portfolio at the end of the period. Applying this concept requires restating the normal performance calculation from a liquidation approach to one involving flows during the period. In other words, pretax performance (assuming for simplicity that all cash flows occur at the end of the period) is normally computed as portfolio ending value plus net withdrawals minus starting value, all divided by the starting value (see Equation 1). From a flow perspective, pretax performance is also the sum of realized capital gains, the difference between unrealized gains at the end and start of the period, and taxable and tax-free income, all divided by the starting value. In this second form, the appropriate tax rates for dividend/interest income and realized capital gains are easy to apply and produce Equation 2. This approach implies, however, that all capital gains were at the discretion of the firm. It represents the client's after-tax performance in an economic sense, after all actual taxes are paid:

$$
\text{Pretax performance} = \frac{\begin{array}{l}\text{Realized gains}\\ + \text{ Increase in unrealized gains during the period}\\ + \text{ Taxable income} + \text{Tax-free income}\end{array}}{\text{Starting asset value}}. \tag{1}
$$

$$
\text{Client after-tax performance} = \frac{\begin{array}{l}\text{Realized gains}(1 - \text{Capital gains tax rate})\\ + \text{ Increase in unrealized gains during the period}\\ + \text{ Taxable income}(1 - \text{Income tax rate})\\ + \text{ Tax-free income}\end{array}}{\text{Starting asset value}}. \tag{2}
$$

In some cases, realized gains in Equation 2 might have to be separately summed for long-term and short-term holding periods and a different capital gains tax rate might have to be applied to each. Note that both taxable and tax-free income in this equation should include accrual of interest and amortization of principal, regardless of whether the income remains in the portfolio, according to standard AIMR practice.

The adjustment proposed here would use Equation 2 for client- or firm-directed withdrawals but add back an adjustment factor (calculated in Equation 3) that reflects both the proportion of assets that the manager had to sell to meet client withdrawals (in excess of income generated during the period) and the unrealized capital gains embedded in the assets at the end of the period. This adjustment term would be added back only if net client withdrawals actually occurred. In other words, it would never be negative.

One way to envision this adjustment is to think of a hypothetical portfolio consisting entirely of assets subject to a tax on withdrawal (e.g., an early withdrawal from an individual retirement account). The adjustment would be the amount of withdrawal times the tax rate. In a real case, on average, only a fraction of the withdrawal is subject to capital gains taxes, namely, the ratio of unrealized gains to the total asset value. At the end of any period, that ratio will equal the sum of unrealized gains and realized gains divided by the sum of ending asset value and net client withdrawals. Thus, the adjustment factor is calculated as

$$\text{Adjustment factor} = \frac{(\text{Capital gains tax rate})(\text{Net client withdrawal})(\text{Realized} + \text{Unrealized gains at end of period})}{(\text{Ending asset value} + \text{Net client withdrawal})} \quad (3)$$

In Equation 3, net client withdrawal equals net withdrawals after subtracting both taxable and tax-free income (and any other positive cash inflows) actually received during the period. Note that income as used in the adjustment factor should be measured on an as-paid basis; that is, it should not include accruals or income not remaining in the portfolio, because those amounts would not be available to meet withdrawals. The firm's after-tax performance, as calculated using Equation 4, thus reflects only the tax effects within the firm's control (which is not to be confused with the client's results after payment of actual taxes).

$$\text{Firm after-tax performance} = \frac{\begin{array}{l}\text{Realized gains } (1 - \text{Capital gains tax rate}) \\ + \text{ Adjustment factor} \\ + \text{ Increase in unrealized gains during the period} \\ + \text{ Taxable income } (1 - \text{Income tax rate}) \\ + \text{ Tax-free income}\end{array}}{\text{Starting asset value}} \quad (4)$$

Benchmarks. The construction of benchmarks appropriate to after-tax composites is a problematic issue because the providers of index statistics do not supply information sufficient to make appropriate after-tax adjustments. AIMR encourages vendors, and encourages managers to request vendors, to develop after-tax benchmarks with disclosure of the methodologies used.

Calculation of a benchmark return is determined by using the actual turnover in the benchmark index. Although those data are not always available for broad indexes, they are currently available for mutual funds, and the methodology is the same. When the information necessary to make the benchmark calculation is not available, the fully liquidated method (i.e., the index and the portfolio are considered fully taxed for both realized and unrealized gains) may provide comparative information that is useful for institutional fixed-income clients, but the inaccuracies of this method are to be disclosed.

The methodology for calculating the after-tax returns of benchmarks is best illustrated by the example in the following case, which uses mutual funds:

Beginning market value (ending market value of previous period)	= $10.00
Capital gains plus dividends per share	= $2.50
Long-term capital gains	= $1.75
Short-term gains and dividend income	= $0.75
Maximum federal long-term capital gains tax rate	= 28.0%
Maximum federal dividend and short-term rate	= 39.6%
Pretax total rate of return	= 30.0%

$10.00 (1 + 30%) = $13.00,

$1.75 (28%) = $0.49,

$0.75 (39.6%) = $0.30,

The after-tax rate of return is calculated as follows:

$$\$13.00 - \$0.49 - \$0.30 = \frac{\$12.21}{\$10.00}$$

$$= 1.221$$

$$= (1.221 - 1.00) \times 100$$

$$= 22.1\%.$$

The after-tax returns for each period would be geometrically linked to produce a cumulative return over longer periods.

Additional shares purchased with previous dividends must be determined to calculate the cost basis of shares in succeeding periods. Using the information above, plus an assumed ending net asset value per share of $12, the calculation of number of ending shares is as follows:

130%($10) = $13,

$13/$12 = 1.083.

The new cost basis is thus 1.083 multiplied by the next year's dividends per share.

This procedure is to be followed for each successive year.

Amortization and Accretion. The impact of amortization and accretion is significant for after-tax performance reporting for tax-exempt bonds. For taxable securities (based on applicable laws and regulations), the impact is reflected as a timing difference and is not necessarily material, particularly for institutions that face the same tax rate for ordinary income as for capital gains.

Amortization of premiums on taxable bonds, if elected, is tax deductible and reduces the tax basis of the security. For tax-exempt bonds, amortization of premiums is required. Usually, no deduction is allowed for tax purposes, but the tax basis of the bonds is still reduced. In the special case of an alternative minimum tax calculation (important to most insurance companies), amortization of the premium can be used to offset tax-exempt income and thus amounts to a partial tax deduction.

Meaningful after-tax performance analysis for original issue discount (OID) tax-exempt bonds, particularly zero-coupon bonds, requires accretion of discount. The effect is to increase income and to increase the tax basis of the security that is producing higher tax-exempt income and lower unrealized (or realized) capital gains. The after-tax performance of tax-exempt zero-coupon bonds may be grossly distorted if the income is not accreted. For tax-exempt bonds purchased after April 30, 1993, the impact of market discount must be considered. For investors who benefit from a lower capital gains rate, the recharacterization of capital gain to ordinary income increases the tax impact.

For taxable securities, OID accretion is subject to income tax. Taxpayers may elect to pay tax on accreted market discount on a current basis or on sale or redemption. Common practice is to defer the tax. Upon sale of a discount security, any amount realized in excess of accreted market discount or accreted OID is subject to the capital gains tax rate.

Real Estate

AIMR recognizes that various alternative forms of private real estate investment are available to real estate investors, including wholly owned real estate, joint venture real estate investments, co-investments, separate accounts, and commingled funds. Investment forms may offer significant differences in financial policies and agreements pertaining to the distribution of earned income to investors and the retention and reinvestment of earned income. In those situations where income is earned at the investment level but is not distributed to investors and, therefore, is retained at the investment level, the accounting policies of some investors may not recognize the earned income unless it is distributed.

Valuations must be performed by independent, objective appraisers with sufficient frequency (not longer than every three years). The appraisers must be asked to originate and communicate value rather than merely confirm prior knowledge. Changes in valuation, including unrealized gains and losses, must be recognized in the reporting period that includes the effective date of the appraisal.

The practice of providing quarterly reports satisfies the quarterly review requirements because the issuance process should include a review of the real estate portfolio, a review of net asset value for financial and performance purposes, and review and disclosure of any factors that might result in a material change to net asset value.

Cash, cash equivalents, and substitute assets (e.g., seller financing) must be combined with real estate assets, and performance returns must be computed and presented on a consolidated basis.

Venture and Private Placements

Problems are inherent in applying the methodology of a time-weighted rate of return as required by the AIMR-PPS standards to investments in venture capital, private limited partnerships, and other private equity investments. Time-weighted rate of return allows the evaluation of investment management skill between any two time periods without regard to the total amount invested at any time during that time period. The measure is independent of the total amount invested because the manager normally does not control the inflow or outflow of money. Selection of the time-weighted methodology is predicated on the assumption that the portfolio investments have total liquidity to accommodate cash flows without distorting the performance results. Neither the liquidity assumptions implicit in the time-weighted rate of return method nor the lack of control over cash flows holds, however, in the case of private equity investments.

Distortions Caused by Liquidity Constraints. Liquidity constraints distort the time-weighted rate of return for venture capital investments and other private placements from several aspects: attribution of investment decisions, cash flow distortion, and pricing bias.

▓ *Attribution of investment decisions*. Secondary markets create liquidity for a public equity portfolio. Money can move in and out of the portfolio, thus changing the investment base from time to time, without the investment firm's control. The time-weighted methodology was created to address the fact that nondiscretionary changes occur in the investment base and should not affect rate-of-return calculations used for comparative performance. In a private equity transaction, control of cash flow is in the investment manager's (general partner's) hands, which negates the need for making time-weighted cash flow adjustments for the purpose of equitable comparisons.

▓ *Cash flow distortion*. The second liquidity issue is more complex. The cash flow pattern inherent in the life cycle of private equity investments may create distortions in a time-weighted rate of return that are not indicative of true investment performance. In partnerships, the initial funding may be used for expenses, which results in a large percentage loss on a small investment base in the first few periods. In some cases, those in which fees use up the entire investment base, the percentage loss can approach 100 percent. A time-weighted methodology in this case, regardless of good performance with later, larger cash flows, would make all subsequently linked returns approximately –100 percent. The time-weighted return may never catch up from the marked valuation decrease and commensurate negative returns in the fund's early life. Thus, time weighting may bias the cumulative return of private equity partnerships when compared with a cumulative dollar-weighted rate of return, which will be more representative of the performance of the total investment during multiple periods.

▓ *Pricing bias*. Unlike in the public markets, no trade-based pricing mechanism exists to determine a period-end value for private market securities. In addition, there are no generally accepted appraisal practices to value private investments at periodic intervals as there are in the real estate market. The usual practice in the private markets is to adjust the partnership's security market values only after some independent market action has occurred, such as the new issue of securities to outside investors, that affects the value of existing securities. Therefore, this sector of the market requires a return calculation that is not affected by interim pricing inaccuracies, as a time-weighted rate of return would be affected.

IRR as the Recommended Calculation Method. The recommended measurement of performance for presentation of the performance of a single private equity investment is the investment's internal rate of return since inception. IRR is superior to a time-weighted rate of return because only cash flows and the closing market value are used in the IRR calculation.

The internal rate of return is the annualized implied discount rate calculated from a series of cash flows. It is the return that equates the present value of all invested capital in an investment to the present value of all returns or the discount rate that will provide a net present value of all cash flows equal to zero. It is formulated as

$$0 = \sum_{i=0}^{n} CF_i \left(1 + \frac{r}{c}\right)^{-(ic)},$$

where

CF = the cash flow for period i (negative for invested capital, positive for distributions or ending-period net asset value)
n = the total number of cash flows
i = period of cash flow
c = number of annual cash flow subperiods; for example, $c = 12$ for monthly cash flows, 4 for quarterly cash flows
r = subperiod internal rate of return or implied discount rate

The subperiod IRR, r, is converted to R (the annualized IRR) by

$$R = (1 + r)^c - 1.$$

The IRR must be calculated using quarterly cash flows ($c = 4$ in the formula) at a minimum. Monthly cash flows are preferred, and daily flows are the most desirable.

Performance Gross or Net of Fees. When a general partner reports historical investment performance, the IRR must be net of expenses, fees, and carry. Gross returns on the fund and on the portfolio investments are recommended as supplemental information.

When a firm reports the results of either separately managed accounts or commingled fund-of-funds structures, the IRR must be reported net of fees, expenses, and carry to the general partner but gross of investment advisory fees, unless results presented net of advisory fees are required to meet applicable regulatory requirements. The AIMR-PPS standards consider that even when net-of-advisory-fee results are not required to meet applicable regulatory requirements, these results provide important supplemental information and should be presented.

When net IRR results are reported, the results must be reduced by fees and expenses regardless of whether these costs are paid from fund assets or from outside the fund.

Net-of-Fees Performance Calculations

Some managers extract a performance-based fee once a year at the end of the year and thus may have difficulty calculating net-of-fees performance figures on a quarterly basis. The problem lies in the fact that the "fee" that is "deducted" from the quarterly figure in this calculation has not actually been removed from the fund. In reality, this "fee" does compound in the fund until the end of the year, when the fee is taken based on the final number. Therefore, a discrepancy exists between the quarterly and annual return figures. This approximation also does not accurately represent the quarterly performance of the manager because only the annual reported number is truly accurate.

Some firms may try to approximate the calculation by simply deducting fees from each gross quarterly number they present. In cases where there is a negative return for a quarter, no adjustment is made and the net number reported is the same as the gross.

The following formula was developed for this situation and yields results that appear to be valid and representative:

With

A = gross yield (as percentage of assets) in Quarter I
B = gross yield (as percentage of assets) in Quarter II
C = gross yield (as percentage of assets) in Quarter III
D = gross yield (as percentage of assets) in Quarter IV
w = net yield (as percentage of assets) in Quarter I
x = net yield (as percentage of assets) in Quarter II
y = net yield (as percentage of assets) in Quarter III
z = net yield (as percentage of assets) in Quarter IV
F = fee ratio as percentage of gross yield, then

$$w = A\,(1 - F) \text{ if } A \geq 0$$

or

$$w = A \text{ if } A < 0;$$

$$x = \frac{(1 - F)(\text{YTD Gross}_2) + 1}{(1 + w)} \text{ if YTD Gross}_2 \geq 0$$

or

$$x = \frac{(1 + \text{YTD Gross}_2) - 1}{1 + w} \text{ if YTD Gross}_2 < 0,$$

where YTD is year to date;

$$y = \frac{(1-F)(\text{YTD Gross}_3) + 1}{(1+w)(1+x)} \quad \text{if YTD Gross}_3 \geq 0$$

or

$$y = \frac{(1+\text{YTD Gross}_3) - 1}{(1+w)(1+x)} \quad \text{if YTD Gross}_3 < 0;$$

$$z = \frac{(1-F)(\text{YTD Gross}_4) + 1}{(1+w)(1+x)(1+y)} \text{if YTD Gross}_4 \geq 0$$

or

$$z = \frac{(1+\text{YTD Gross}_4) - 1}{(1+w)(1+x)(1+y)} \quad \text{if YTD Gross}_4 < 0.$$

For example: Manager Q expects a 20 percent ($F = 20$) fee at the end of the year if his fund has a positive annualized gross yield. Table 1 compares the net yield of Manager Q's fund with funds that exact the management fee quarterly: Manager Q's true annualized net return would be

$(1 - F)$ (Annualized gross return) $(1 - 0.2)$ $(98.02) = 78.42$.

Table 1. Yield Comparison for Funds with Annual versus Quarterly Fees

Quarter	Manager Q's Fund				Black Index	
	Gross Yield	YTD Gross Yield	Net Yield (by old method)	YTD Yield (by old method)	Net Yield	YTD Net Yield
I	17.96%	17.96%	14.37%	14.37%	14.37%	14.37%
II	−32.47	−20.34	−32.47	−22.77	−30.35	−20.34
III	105.32	63.55	84.26	42.31	89.36	50.84
IV	21.07	98.02	16.86	66.31	18.28	78.42

3. Presentation of Results

This chapter outlines the required and recommended AIMR-PPS standards for presenting investment performance results in compliance with the Standards. Any information beyond the required presentation items that can help meet the goals of fair representation and full disclosure should also be presented in the form of supplemental information.

Requirements

1. General

   a. A 10-year performance record (or a record for the period since firm inception if inception is less than 10 years) must be presented.

   b. Annual returns for all years must be presented. Performance for periods of less than one year must not be annualized.

   c. Composite results may not be restated following changes in a firm's organization.

   d. Composites must include only assets under management and may not link simulated or model portfolios with actual performance.

   e. For composites containing portfolios that use leverage:

      • If the use of leverage is discretionary, the performance presented must include the effects of the leverage. Performance on a restated, all-cash basis (i.e., removing the effect of the leverage from the return) must also be provided.

      • If the use of leverage is nondiscretionary (i.e., mandated by the client), performance must be presented on an all-cash basis.

   f. Performance results of a past firm or affiliation must not be used to represent the historical record of a new affiliation or a new firm entity.

2. International

   If a stand-alone composite is formed using subsectors from multiple composites, its return must be presented with:

      • a list of the underlying composites from which the subsector was drawn *and*

- the percentage of each composite the subsector represents.

3. Real Estate

   Returns from income and capital appreciation must be presented in addition to total return.

4. Venture and Private Placements

   a. General partners

      - Cumulative IRR must be presented since inception of the fund.

      - Presentation of return information must be in a vintage-year format.

   b. Intermediaries and investment advisors

      - For separately managed accounts and commingled fund-of-funds structures, cumulative IRR must be presented since inception.

      - The inclusion of all discretionary pooled fund-of-funds and separately managed portfolios in composites must be defined by vintage year.

      - For calculating composite returns, the IRR must be based on an aggregation of all the appropriate partnership cash flows into one IRR calculation—as if from one investment.

5. Wrap-Fee Accounts

   Wrap-fee performance must be shown net of all fees charged directly or indirectly to the account (unless transaction expenses can be determined and deducted).

Recommendations

1. General

   a. Composite performance should be presented gross of investment management fees and before taxes (except for international withholding taxes).

   b. Equal-weighted composite results should be presented as supplemental information.

   c. Supplemental information the firm deems valuable should be presented.

2. International

    For presentations of returns excluding currency (e.g., for attribution purposes), local currency returns should be calculated using spot rates and hedged returns should be calculated using forward rates.

3. Taxable Clients

    If returns are presented after taxes, client-specific tax rates may be used for each portfolio (but composite performance should be based on the same tax rate for all clients in the composite). The following presentations should be made for composites:

    -   beginning and ending market values,
    -   contributions and withdrawals,
    -   beginning and ending unrealized capital gains,
    -   realized short-term and long-term capital gains,
    -   taxable income and tax-exempt income,
    -   the accounting convention used for the treatment of realized capital gains (e.g., highest cost, average cost, lowest cost, FIFO, LIFO), and
    -   the method or source for computing after-tax benchmark return (if a benchmark is shown).

4. Real Estate

    a. Equity ownership investment strategies should be presented separately.

    b. When presenting the components of total return, recognition of income at the investment level, rather than at the operating level, is preferred.

5. Wrap-Fee Accounts

    Pure gross-of-fees performance should be reported (in addition to the required net-of-fees performance), but gross-of-fees performance should be presented only to prospective wrap-fee clients.

Leverage

Firms must disclose the presence of leverage and/or derivatives in portfolios. The disclosure discussion must contain sufficient detail that current or prospective clients can understand the pattern of returns and the risks from the leverage or derivatives positions.

Where leverage is straightforward (such as buying stocks on margin, buying futures in an already fully invested account, or managing futures overlay strategies) and the strategy would be replicable in the securities markets but for the lack of sufficient cash in the portfolio, the results must be recalculated to an all-cash basis. If the client's mandate for the account has given the manager discretion to apply the leverage, the actual rate of return (without adjusting the denominator for the effect of the leverage) should be included in the composite. The composite results with all leveraged accounts restated to an all-cash basis (with the denominator increased to reflect the actual leverage used) must also be presented. If, alternatively, the client mandate requires the leverage position, the all-cash return must be included in the composite results.

Where leverage is obtained by means that involve options or other derivatives and/or trading processes that deliver nonsymmetrical patterns of returns, no restatement to an all-cash basis should be done because the results could not be replicated simply by reason of having additional cash available to invest in securities.

In determining the assets of a firm and the assets of individual composites or accounts:

- If leverage is discretionary to the manager by client mandate, the firm's assets and the total assets used in the composites should include only the actual cash amount under management. The maximum amount of leverage allowed by the client should be reported separately as an overlay strategy.
- If leverage is required by the client, the firm's and composite's assets must include the account size increased to reflect the degree of required leverage.

Model Portfolios

Composites must include only assets under management and may not link simulated and model portfolios with actual performance. Model performance results may be presented to a potential client as supplementary information, but the model results must be clearly identified as such and must not be linked to actual results.

Gross versus Net of Fees

The AIMR-PPS standards recommend that performance be presented gross of management fees. If law or regulation requires otherwise, however, the applicable law or regulation is to be followed and reporting the gross-of-fees performance is recommended as supplemental information. If a net-of-fees calculation is used, because of laws or regulations, the firm must disclose the method used and include a fee schedule.

When net-of-fees composite results are shown, the firm must also disclose the weighted-average fee to enable a prospective client to compute composite performance on a gross-of-fees basis.

The AIMR-PPS standards recommend that performance results be presented gross of fees because a firm's fee schedule is usually scaled to size of assets. Therefore, performance results after deduction of an average management fee will not be representative of results for a portfolio that is much larger or much smaller than the size of the portfolio represented by the average fee. It is more representative to show results before the deduction of management fees and provide a fee schedule that represents the fee that would actually be paid by the prospective client.

In addition, because fees are sometimes negotiable, presenting performance gross of fees shows the firm's expertise in managing assets without the impact of the firm's or clients' negotiating skills.

The U.S. Securities and Exchange Commission (SEC) staff allows performance information to be presented gross of management fees in one-on-one presentations if accompanied by disclosures that

- the results do not reflect the deduction of investment management fees;
- the client's return will be reduced by the management fees and any other expenses incurred in the management of the account;
- the advisor's investment advisory fees are described in Part II of the advisor's Form ADV.

Also accompanying these disclosures must be "a representative example" that shows the effect an investment advisory fee, compounded over a period of years, could have on the total value of a client's portfolio. The SEC staff defines one-on-one presentations as manager performance presentations to any client, prospective client, consultant, or affiliated group entrusted to consider manager selection and retention. Communications by firms can, therefore, be made to multiple representatives of a given prospect even if the group represents several portfolios. Any written performance presentation material distributed to more than one client or prospect in other than one-on-one presentations, however, must present performance results after deduction of management fees.

Differences in performance results occur when portfolio performance is reported gross of management fees rather than net of management fees. An example using three periods, 1, 2, and 10 years, can illustrate what happens when total return is computed gross of fees and net of fees: Assume a portfolio that has a steady investment return, gross of fees, of 0.5 percent per month and total management fees of 0.05 percent per month of the market value of the portfolio on the last day of the month. Management fees are deducted from the market value of the portfolio on that day. There are no cash flows during the period.

In this simple situation, the value of the portfolio gross of fees at the end of any month $i(GMV_i)$ is given by the formula

$$GMV_i = MV_{START}\,(1 + RGOF_i\,)^i,$$

where MV_{START} is the market value of the portfolio at the start of the period and GOF_i is the gross-of-fees monthly investment return.

The value of the portfolio net of management fees for any month $i(NMV_i)$ is its value after such fees are deducted. The quantity is given by

$$NMV_i = NMV_{i-1}(1 + RGOF)(1 - F),$$

where NMV_{i-1} is the market value, less management fees, of the portfolio at the end of the previous month and F is the fee rate, expressed as a proportion.

Because fees are tied to the market value of the portfolio, this equation simply states that the value (net of fees) for the portfolio is last month's net-of-fees value times this month's growth. This result is multiplied by a factor $(1 - F)$ that reduces it by the amount of this month's management fees.

For the first month of the period, then, the net-of-fees market value is

$$NMV_1 = MV_{START}\,(1 + RGOF)(1 - F).$$

The value for the second month of the period is

$$NMV_2 = NMV_1\,(1 + RGOF)(1 - F)$$
$$= [MV_{START}\,(1 + RGOF)(1 - F)](1 + RGOF)(1 - F)$$
$$= MV_{START}\,(1 + RGOF)^2(1 - F)^2.$$

The general formula for computing the market value of the example portfolio, net of fees, for any month i is

$$NMV_i = MV_{START}\,(1 + RGOF)^i(1 - F)^i.$$

Given these formulas, calculating the total return, gross versus net of fees, for any period is a simple matter: Total return for the period ending with month i, assuming no cash flows, is

$$R_{TOTAL} = \frac{MV_i - MV_{START}}{MV_{START}},$$

where MV_i is GMV_i or NMV_i depending on whether the calculation is of total return gross or net of fees.

In the example, the return before fees, $RGOF$, is 0.5 percent (0.005) and the fee rate, F, is 0.05 percent (0.0005). When these values are used, the total returns, gross and net of fees, for 1, 2, and 10 years (i.e., 12, 24, and 120 months) are as shown in Table 2.

Table 2. Gross-of-Fees versus Net-of-Fees Example

Period (years)	Total Return		Basis Points Differential
	Gross of Fees	Net of Fees	
1	6.17%	5.54%	63
2	12.72	11.38	134
10	81.94	71.39	1,055

Table 2 shows that the total return during the first two years is 134 basis points lower when performance is presented net of fees. By the end of the 10th year, this difference has grown to more than 1,000 basis points. The magnitude of the difference between gross-of-fees and net-of-fees returns will depend on a variety of factors; this example is purposely simplified, but it illustrates the marked difference in total return that the two ways of presenting results can yield. It also shows that, assuming other factors such as investment return and fees remain constant, the difference increases because of the compounding effect over time.

If an investment management firm reduces its management fee charged to clients, for any number of reasons, the recommended method is to waive the appropriate portion of the management fee so that neither a withdrawal nor deposit of cash (i.e., payment or refund of fees) occurs. A reduction in fee should not be treated as income to the separate account, which will erroneously inflate performance. Because the "fee rebate" is not generated as income or capital of the portfolio, it has no influence on performance results.

In a net-of-fees calculation, when fees are paid from the corpus of the fund, the payments should be included as a withdrawal of capital in F (flows) and in FW (weighted flows). In addition, performance results are reduced by deducting fees as negative income in the numerator. Using the modified Dietz method for illustration (see Chapter 2), the net-of-fees return is

$$R = \frac{MVE - MVB - F - FEES}{MVB + FW}.$$

In this example, MVE (which includes accrued income for the period) is reduced by the fees. Because fees have been paid out of the account, they should be treated the same as any other negative flow or withdrawal. In other words, F includes the (negative) fee payment. The fees now need to be deducted from the numerator to reduce the gross return to a net return.

When the fee is paid by an external source, the fee must be subtracted from only the numerator because it has not reduced MVE or been included in the calculation of F. This calculation has the same impact of reducing investment earnings by the amount of the fee without making any cash flow adjustment.

Pretax Reporting

The AIMR-PPS standards recommend gross-of-taxes performance for the presentation of results to prospective clients. Gross-of-taxes presentation allows prospective clients with taxable assets to estimate after-tax results based on tax rates appropriate to their individual circumstances. The client's specific information is needed to make the estimates. Gross-of-taxes reporting is also preferred because of the complexities of presenting after-tax performance in a meaningful and comparable way within the constraints of current systems.

Pretax reporting does not, however, show how successful a manager has been in applying an investment style or strategy to meet the tax requirements of specific clients. It also overstates multiyear performance because of the implied compounding. For example, a 10 percent pretax annual return compounded for 10 years is 159 percent, but when converted to an 8 percent annual after-tax return, the compounded 10-year return is only 116 percent.

For the reporting of pretax total returns of taxable portfolios that include both tax-exempt and taxable bonds, the AIMR-PPS standards recommend that income on tax-exempt bonds *not* be grossed up to a pretax basis. Therefore, a total rate of return for the composite should be presented without adjustment for tax-exempt income to a pretax basis. As supplemental information, the manager could show an after-tax total rate of return for the composite by applying the federal tax rates to the taxable portion rather than by grossing up the tax-exempt portion.

Partial-Year Returns

Performance for periods of less than one year may not be annualized. Partial-year returns may be disclosed as partial-year returns provided the period covered is clearly noted. For example, if a manager has returns for three full quarters and 2 months, the manager may show only an 11-month return.

Portability

Performance is the record of the firm, not of the individual. The AIMR-PPS standards state that performance results of a prior firm may not be used to represent the historical record of a new affiliation or a newly formed entity. Using the performance data from a prior firm or affiliation as supplemental information is permitted as long as the past record is identified clearly as such and is not linked to the results of the new affiliation.

Changes in a firm's organization should not lead to alteration of composite results. Therefore, composites should include all accounts managed by a member of a firm, even if the individual responsible for the past results is no longer with the firm, and composites should not include portfolios managed by members of the firm before they joined the firm.

Performance data from a prior firm can be used, with the proper disclosures, as supplemental information. The manager must give credit for the performance to the prior affiliation and describe his or her responsibilities at the previous employer. If the responsibilities are accurately portrayed, the market will determine how the record should be interpreted in light of the new affiliation or entity. The historical results of the previous affiliation cannot be linked with the results of the new affiliation or newly formed entity. The nonlinking of records is a key factor.

When a firm is acquired by another firm, the historical record is that of the acquiring firm; that is, the acquiring firm can show the performance results of the acquired firm as supplemental information but cannot claim that past record as its own.

When acquired accounts are to be incorporated into the investment style and strategy of the acquiring firm, they should be treated as new accounts and placed in a composite labeled "acquisition of XYZ" until the assets can be blended over time into existing composites that meet compliance requirements. The acquiring firm will need to set reasonable, consistently applied, documented criteria for determining when the acquired assets complete the transition to the new style. Some accounts will be modified more quickly than others. Therefore, rather than setting one arbitrary time frame for bringing all acquired assets into existing composites that meet compliance requirements, different portfolios can transition at different times as long as the criteria are consistently followed. The historical performance records for these strategies will be those of the acquiring firm, and even though the strategies have been discontinued, the acquiring firm must disclose the availability of the records of the acquired firm and provide the records when requested.

When a firm is purchased for the purpose of bringing on staff and resources to offer a product specific to the acquired firm but new to the acquiring firm, the rules of portability apply. If substantially all the investment decision makers and substantially all the assets come with the acquired firm, and if the staff and decision-making process remain intact and independent, then

- the performance record of the acquired firm for that product can be shown as the performance record of the acquiring firm and can be linked to ongoing results consistent with the composite creation guidelines of the AIMR-PPS standards *and*
- when the investment style and strategy of the acquired firm is to be maintained and its accounts represent separate composites, the assets of the acquired firm must meet the requirements as of the first full reporting period one year after the acquisition date in order for a firm to claim compliance, which creates a one-year period for bringing the acquired assets into compliance.

For example, if the assets are acquired in mid-July, the assets would need to meet compliance requirements as of the beginning of the fourth quarter of the following year. The historical performance records for the strategies will be those of the acquired firm. If the staff of the two merged firms are combined and the decision making is shared, the performance record of the acquired firm should be presented as supplemental information and must not be linked to ongoing results.

When an acquisition is made, it is recommended, but not required, that the acquiring firm disclose the amount of assets and the number of portfolios involved. As the new assets are brought into compliance, prospective clients will see an increase in the size of assets and number of portfolios through the required composite disclosures. Therefore, full disclosure of acquisitions is in the best interests of both the prospective client and the acquiring firm.

The use of a predecessor's performance could be misleading if one or more individuals other than those at the successor organization played a role in the prior firm's strategy (such as other investment committee members), security selection (such as research analysts), or trading if trading strategies were integral to the firm's overall investment strategy.

Portability of prior investment results can be applied to the merged results of commingled funds—that is, when two commingled funds are merged into one—according to the full disclosure requirements of the Standards. Disclosure must be made that the surviving fund is a combination of Fund X and Fund Y. The manager must determine which is the "surviving" fund (i.e., which fund represents continuity in investment process). Portability of that record as the historical record will depend on whether investment process, investment objective, and investment advisor and the advisor's staff remain the same. Continuity requirements for linking the historical record to the ongoing record of the merged fund are the same as for the general portability guidelines of the Standards: The record of the "nonsurviving" fund must be made available upon request, and if the investment process is changed, or if the investment staff changes, the historical records of each of the merged funds must be presented and cannot be linked to the ongoing record of the merged fund.

Investment firms are required to keep all documents (confirmations, statements, etc.) that are necessary to form the basis for or demonstrate the calculation of the performance or rate of return (current and historical performance results) of any or all managed accounts that the advisor uses in advertisements. Therefore, the firm must have the documents for each year that an advisor is showing performance results, however many years that may be, and for all portfolios that are included in the performance results.

If a newly formed entity constitutes a change in name or ownership only—that is, all previous decision makers have transferred to the new entity, substantially all client assets have transferred, access to research records remains the same, and the management of the new firm is confident that there will be no misrepresentation in presenting the record of the previous firm as representing the historical record of the new entity—the guideline of "the record belongs to the firm" applies. In this instance, the record would stay with the firm that has simply undergone a change in name or ownership only.

Supplemental Information

The AIMR-PPS standards recommend that the firm present supplemental information the firm deems valuable to prospective and current clients. Such disclosures might include the average market capitalization of stocks within a composite, the average quality and duration of bond holdings, and other additional information recommended by the Standards. This information must not supplant the required information, and it must be accompanied by the appropriate composite returns.

The inclusion of attribution as supplementary information in presentations is encouraged. Because different methodologies for calculating attribution can lead to different results, attribution analysis should be accompanied by a clear explanation of the methodology used.

Multiple-Asset Composite Segments

When a firm uses the total return of a multiple-asset composite to market a multiple-asset portfolio strategy, cash allocation to each of the segments of the multiple-asset composite is not required. When a firm uses the total return of a multiple-asset composite to market a multiple-asset portfolio strategy but the firm wishes to present the segment returns of the multiple-asset composite as supplemental information, the segment returns may be shown without making a cash allocation as long as the returns for each of the composite's segments (including the cash segment) are shown along with the composite's total return.

International

If a stand-alone composite is formed using subsectors from multiple composites, its return must be presented with a list of the underlying composites from which the subsector was drawn, together with the percentage of each composite the subsector represents. If the subsector is not treated as a separate entity, the subsector-only performance may be provided only as supplemental information to the composite or composites from which the subsector was drawn. The presentation of subsector results as supplemental information may be based on representative portfolios, however, as long as this approach is disclosed. Carve-outs presented as supplemental information must not be combined with stand-alone portfolios.

When expressing the return of a portfolio excluding the effect of currency, the return should be shown fully hedged back to the base currency of that portfolio. The reason is that the investor cannot actually achieve the local return of a market that is denominated in a currency different from the portfolio's base currency, whereas achieving the hedged return is possible. If this hedged return is not calculated, disclosure must be made that the return is in the local currency and does not account for interest rate differentials in forward currency exchange rates.

The total return from currency can be closely approximated by taking the percentage difference (i.e., geometric difference) between the total return in base currency and the total return in local currency. A more accurate method, however, is to take the percentage difference between the total in base currency and the total fully hedged into base currency, if this information is available.

Real Estate

Because of its unique characteristics, particularly the lack of a readily verifiable secondary market to determine asset values, real estate performance presentation guidelines warrant separate treatment. For real estate investments, the attribution and separate presentation of returns from income and capital appreciation, in addition to total returns, is required. Appreciation includes realized and unrealized gains and losses. Income is equivalent to net investment income (before or after investment management fees, as applicable), and income is determined by generally accepted accounting principles (GAAP).

For the purpose of performance reporting, real estate mortgages with fixed or variable interest rates are considered fixed-income securities. Participation and convertible mortgages (i.e., hybrid mortgages) are considered real estate investments.

In presentations of the components of total return, the recognition of income at the investment level is preferred over recognition of income at the operating level. The term "investment level" is intended to be synonymous with the term "investor level." Therefore, all income and expenses from real estate investment programs (short-term interest income, appraisal, legal, accounting, cash management, and banking charges; portfolio management, asset management, and investment management fees; corporate or fund-level expenses; and reporting expenses) are included in the return calculations. As outlined in Exhibit 2, the concept of investment level is distinct from the operating or property level, the returns from which may exclude some or all of the nonproperty investment income and expenses.

Exhibit 2. Summary of Differences between Property-and Investment-Level Returns

Property-Level Returns	Investment-Level Returns
Returns are primarily based on the cash invested in a property (at acquisition plus subsequent capitalized expenditures), recognized changes in value, and principal payments on debt.	Returns are based on the total equity of the investors in the investment program.
Net income is accrual-basis net income at the property level (which would ultimately be consolidated into the investment program's net income).	Net income is accrual-basis net income for the consolidated investment program as reported in the financial statements.
Net income is not considered to be retained by the property, so it does not have to be "earned on" (does not affect the denominator).	Net income is retained by the investment program, is included in the denominator, and must be "earned on."
Recognized appreciation/depreciation (realized and unrealized) affects the denominator and must be earned on.	Recognized appreciation/depreciation (realized and unrealized) affects the denominator and must be earned on.
Capital expenditures affect the denominator and must be earned on.	Capital expenditures have no effect on the denominator.
Capital contributions by investors have no effect on the return calculation.	Capital contributions affect equity; therefore, they are weighted into the denominator based on actual days.
Cash distributions to investors have no effect on the return calculation.	Cash distributions affect equity; therefore, they are weighted into the denominator based on actual days.

Venture and Private Placement

Three different constituencies within the venture market are affected by the performance presentation requirements of the AIMR-PPS standards:

- current and prospective clients of investment advisors and current and potential investors of fund raisers in limited partnerships,
- the general partner of a limited partnership (or fund raiser) who solicits investment in a limited partnership from potential investors and then has sole discretion over the investment of the proceeds, and
- the investment advisor or intermediary who recommends or selects partnership participation for investments.

The time-weighted (rather than the dollar-weighted) rate-of-return methodology is the industry standard for calculating comparative performance of portfolios of publicly traded securities. However, time-weighted return may not properly reflect the performance of private equity investments. The calculation method recommended for private equity investments is thus the dollar-weighted rate of return, which allows current and prospective clients to compare the results of these investments. However, it is inappropriate to compare returns calculated for publicly traded securities, and it is recommended that firms include in their disclosures that such comparisons may be misleading.

Wrap Fees

For portfolios in which different types of fees are embedded in a single fee, as in the case of wrap-fee or all-in accounts, the firm must present performance net of all fees charged directly or indirectly unless actual transaction costs are determinable. Estimated transaction costs are not permitted.

Wrap fees include advisory fees, transaction costs, and fees for other services. Wrap-fee accounts are unique and significantly different from traditional brokerage or investment management relationships because a single fee is charged for several combined services. The fees for various services are difficult to unbundle. As a result, the AIMR-PPS standards *require* the presentation of net-of-fees performance to wrap-fee prospects and *recommend* the further presentation of gross-of-all-fees performance to wrap-fee prospects unless prohibited by applicable law. The Standards also recommend that wrap-fee composites be presented only to prospective wrap-fee clients.

When wrap-fee composites are presented to prospective wrap-fee clients, the composites may include portfolios managed according to the same style or strategy that do not meet the wrap-fee definition only if performance results are reported after the deduction of the maximum wrap fee included in the composite, less actual, determinable transaction costs. Portfolios included in a wrap-fee composite that do not meet the wrap-fee definition must disclose for each year presented (1) the dollar amount of assets represented and (2) the fee deducted.

When composites are presented to clients other than prospective wrap-fee clients, if a composite is presented gross of fees and includes portfolios meeting the wrap-fee definition, those portfolios must be presented either net of all fees or net of actual transaction costs. Appropriate disclosures are mandatory, including fees, size, and style. Gross-of-fees returns may not include transaction costs.

4. Disclosures

To be in compliance with the AIMR-PPS standards, an investment firm must provide the required disclosures for each period the firm presents composite performance. Additional disclosures may be needed to meet the objectives of fair representation and full disclosure. The disclosures are expected to be specific to each circumstance and, therefore, may not be required in all situations.

Requirements

To be in compliance with the AIMR-PPS standards, a firm's presentation of its investment performance must disclose the following information:

1. General

   For all composites, a performance presentation must disclose:

   - the availability of a complete list and description of the firm's composites,
   - the number of portfolios and amount of assets in a composite and the percentage of the firm's total assets the composite represents,
   - the definition of "firm" used to determine the firm's total assets and firmwide compliance,
   - whether balanced portfolio segments are included in single-asset composites and an explanation of how cash has been allocated among asset segments,
   - whether performance results are calculated gross or net of investment management fees, what the firm's fee schedule is, and for net results, the average weighted management fee,
   - the existence of a minimum asset size below which portfolios are excluded from a composite,
   - a measure of the dispersion of individual component portfolio returns around the aggregate composite return,
   - whether settlement-date valuation is used rather than trade-date valuation,
   - the inclusion of any non-fee-paying portfolios in composites and included in the definition of total firm assets,
   - the use and extent of leverage, including a description of the use, frequency, and characteristics of any derivatives used,

- a material change in personnel responsible for investment management,
- the effective date of firm compliance, and
- for historical performance records prior to the applicable effective date,
  - the performance that is not in compliance with the requirements of the AIMR-PPS standards and
  - a description of how noncompliance periods are out of compliance.

2. International

   The performance presentation must disclose:

   - whether composites and benchmarks are presented gross or net of withholding taxes on dividends, interest, and capital gains; if net, the assumed tax rate for both the composite and the benchmark,
   - whether the composite is a subsector of a larger portfolio and, if so, the percentage of the larger portfolio the subsector represents,
   - whether representative portfolios are used in the returns of subsectors shown as supplemental information,
   - for composites managed against specific benchmarks, the percentage of the composites invested in countries or regions not included in the benchmark, and
   - for returns that exclude the effect of currency, whether the returns are presented in local currency and, if so, a statement that the local currency return does not account for interest rate differentials in forward currency exchange rates.

3. Taxable Clients

   The performance presentation must disclose:

   - for composites of taxable portfolios, the composite assets as a percentage of total assets in taxable portfolios (including nondiscretionary assets) managed according to the same strategy for the same type of client,
   - the tax rate assumptions if performance results are presented after taxes, and

- both client average and manager average performance if adjustments are made for nondiscretionary cash withdrawals.

4. Real Estate

   The performance presentation must disclose:

   - the absence of independent appraisals,
   - the source of the valuation and the valuation policy,
   - total fee structure and its relationship to asset valuation,
   - the return formula and accounting policies for such items as capital expenditures, tenant improvements, and leasing commissions,
   - the cash distribution and retention policy,
   - whether the returns
     - are based on audited operating results,
     - exclude any investment expense that may be paid by the investors, or
     - include interest income from short-term cash investments or other related investments, and
   - the cash distribution and retention policies with regard to income earned at the investment level.

5. Venture and Private Placements

   a. For general partners, the performance presentation must disclose:

      - changes in the general partner since inception of fund,
      - type of investment, and
      - investment strategy.

   b. For intermediaries and investment advisors, the performance presentation must disclose:

      - the number of portfolios and funds included in the vintage-year composite,
      - composite assets,
      - composite assets in each vintage year as a percentage of total firm assets (discretionary and nondiscretionary committed capital), and
      - composite assets in each vintage year as a percentage of total private equity assets.

6. Wrap-Fee Accounts

   a. When a firm presents portfolios included in a wrap-fee composite that do not meet the wrap-fee definition, the firm must disclose for each year presented:

      - the dollar amount of assets represented *and*
      - the fee deducted.

   b. When wrap-fee composite returns are presented before fees, the performance presentation must disclose:

      - fees,
      - investment style, and
      - the information that "pure" gross-of-fees return does not include transaction costs.

Recommendations

Following are the recommended additional disclosures to fully meet the spirit and intent of fair representation and full disclosure in compliance with the AIMR-PPS standards:

1. General

   For all composites, a performance presentation should disclose:

   a. volatility of the aggregate composite return,

   b. benchmarks that parallel the risk or investment style the composite is expected to track,

   c. differences in portfolio structure relative to the designated benchmarks,

   d. cumulative composite returns for all periods, and

   e. portfolio size range for each composite (unless portfolios are five or fewer) and the percentage of total assets managed in the same asset class as represented by the composite.

2. International

   a. For composites, performance presentation should disclose:

      - the range or the average country weights of a composite that is managed against a specific benchmark and
      - inconsistencies among portfolios within a composite in the treatment of exchange rates.

   b. For presentations of returns excluding the effect of currency (e.g., for attribution purposes), whether the return is the hedged return (using forward rates) or the local return (using spot rates) should be specified. Local returns should be accompanied by a statement that the local return is in local currency and does not account for interest rate differentials in forward currency exchange rates.

3. Venture and Private Placements

   a. For general partners, the following should be disclosed:

      • gross IRR (before fees, expenses, and carry), which should be used at the fund and the portfolio level, as supplemental information,

      • the multiple on committed capital net of fees and carry to the limited partners,

      • the multiple on invested capital gross of fees and carry,

      • the distribution multiple on paid-in capital net of fees to the limited partners, and

      • the residual multiple on paid-in capital net of fees and carry to the limited partners.

   b. Intermediaries and investment advisors

      The number and size should be expressed in terms of committed capital of discretionary and nondiscretionary consulting clients.

The AIMR-PPS standards require, at a minimum, presentation of performance on an annual basis. As long as prospective clients have received past results that were in compliance with the required disclosures within a 12-month period, firms may present interim data and returns (i.e., "flash numbers") without quarterly disclosures. Firms should state that a full presentation in compliance with the Standards is available upon request. If a prospective client is receiving investment results for the first time, the required disclosures must be included *or* must accompany a flash report.

List of Composites

A performance presentation should disclose the availability of a complete list and description of the firm's composites. Except on request, a firm need not individually list the single-portfolio composites. For these composites, an acceptable presentation would be to simply state on the firm's list of composites the number of such unique portfolios, the total assets represented by these portfolios, and the percentage of firm assets they represent. The firm must also include a brief description of the strategies that typify these portfolios, such as "global portfolios managed to very specific benchmarks." The performance results of any of the single-portfolio composites must be made available to prospective clients.

For composites of five or fewer portfolios, the disclosure "five or fewer portfolios" may be made rather than a disclosure of the exact number of portfolios. When disclosing the number of portfolios included in the composite's annual return, the amount of composite assets, and composite assets as a percentage of firm assets, the manager may choose to report the number of portfolios as of the beginning of the period or as of the end of the period. The method must be followed consistently across time periods.

Risk

Risk should be clearly understood as being multiple and uncertain in nature, duration, and impact. What risks should be disclosed to prospective and current clients is difficult to define precisely; the types of risks are practically limitless. The use of a variety of measures with an understanding of their shortcomings will provide the most valuable information because no one statistic can consistently capture all the elements of risk of an asset class or a style of management.

Risk disclosures should facilitate comparison among a broad range of investment vehicles but must be appropriate to the investment strategy represented by a composite. The best measures do not allow a firm to manipulate the measure to the firm's advantage, are relatively easy to interpret, and apply uniformly to all firms.

It is very important not to confuse risk with volatility; they are not synonymous. Volatility measures, which relate to the total variability of actual returns (e.g., beta), indicate the risk of having returns different from that particular benchmark or index. This type of risk is only one of many.

The AIMR-PPS standards recommend that both total (absolute) and market (relative) risks be presented in conjunction with composite returns. Total risk relates to the variability of actual (absolute) returns not relative to the market. Market (systematic) risk relates to the volatility of returns relative to the market or some other benchmark. Thus, total risk addresses the level of absolute returns over time (and perhaps safety in the case of a money market fund compared with a speculative equity fund), whereas market or systematic risk addresses the pattern of returns relative to the market over time.

Risk Measures. Risk measures represent the riskiness of investment strategies and include standard deviation across time, beta, duration, and others that are based on current and historical data.

Benchmarks, including market indexes, manager universes, and normal portfolios, provide a relative measure for the riskiness of a strategy.

Investment Strategy Risk. Volatility measures are used to gauge an element of the risk of an investment strategy, namely, return volatility over time. Clearly, however, no one measure can capture all elements of the riskiness of a strategy. A variety of measures can be used to assist investors in understanding absolute or relative risk. The most common measures are historical representations and provide a framework for understanding expected risk of volatility given historical experience. None of the risk measures is a *predictor* of expected risk or volatility. Moreover, there is a trade-off between risk and return. A manager who earned 15 percent is not necessarily better than a manager who earned 14 percent if the former took more risk than the latter.

▨ *Standard deviation.* Standard deviation of portfolio performance over time is a measure of the variability or dispersion of historical returns around their central tendency or mean return. It is the most common measure of volatility other than simple high–low range. Standard deviation attempts to measure how much exposure to volatility was taken historically in implementing an investment strategy. Whether this volatility equates to risk depends on the particular investor's objectives for the time horizon in question. Theoretically, a composite with a higher (or lower) standard deviation than its benchmark index or category is more (or less) risky, and this riskiness is compensated for by the composite having a higher (or lower) return potential. Standard deviation is also a useful measure of the relative volatility of fund categories.

The measure has its limitations, however. Volatility may not be correlated with risk. Furthermore, historical volatility may not be the same for the future as it was in the past, particularly if the portfolio manager, investment strategy, or market conditions change. Also, time-period-selection bias can be a problem for short or nonparallel periods. Finally, standard deviation assumes that data (returns in this case) are normally distributed—that is, that they have similar means and are distributed in a bell-shaped pattern—but these assumptions are often not true. If the limitations of standard deviation are clearly articulated and understood, however, the measure can be valuable in evaluating one form of risk—volatility.

The standard deviation of historical data for an asset-weighted composite over time, S_P, is calculated as follows[1]:

$$S_p = \sqrt{\frac{\Sigma[C_{ASSET_i} - MEAN(C_{ASSET})]^2}{n}} \, ,$$

where C_{ASSET_i} is the asset-weighted composite return in the *i*th time period and *n* is the number of periods in the study.

This type of standard deviation as an external measure of volatility of composite returns across time can be annualized as long as the numbers are reasonably independent and normally distributed and the number of data points is sufficient. The annualized standard deviation in this case would be the quarterly standard deviation multiplied by the square root of 4. If monthly returns are used, the monthly standard deviation would be multiplied by the square root of 12. If monthly or quarterly returns are not random (i.e., the returns are trending or reverting to the mean), the annualized standard deviation may differ depending on whether monthly or quarterly returns are used.

■ *Beta*. Beta measures the sensitivity (volatility) of a composite's returns relative to its benchmark (index) return. It attempts to deter-

---

[1]The use of *n* in the denominator of standard deviation (as opposed to *n* − 1) is supported because using *n* yields the maximum likelihood estimate of standard deviation. The use of *n* − 1 in the denominator of sample variance makes sample variance, s^2, an unbiased estimate of the true variance, σ^2. When the square root of s^2 is taken to obtain the sample standard deviation, *s*, however, the result is not an unbiased estimate of population standard deviation, σ. The seldom-used unbiased estimate of standard deviation has a cumbersome constant based on sample size, which needs to be calculated. Because the unbiased estimate of standard deviation is not practical, it is wise to use the maximum likelihood estimate of standard deviation.

Further compounding the issue is the fact that the use of *n* − 1 (unbiased) hinges on the assumptions that random and independent samples are taken from a normal distribution. The sample data (in this case, the manager's returns) are not random, arguably not independent, and may not be normally distributed.

mine whether the composite is incurring more (or less) risk relative to the benchmark. The significance of beta is that it measures relative market (systematic) risk (as opposed to total risk). Like standard deviation, a beta higher than 1.0 in a composite indicates, theoretically, that the composite has greater-than-market volatility, which should result in higher-than-market returns in a rising market and lower-than-market returns in a falling market. A beta lower than 1.0 indicates volatility lower than the market, which should result in lower-than-market returns in a rising market and "less negative" returns than the market in a falling market.

Beta has the same basic limitations as standard deviation, but when these limitations are understood, it is often a useful proxy for market risks in a portfolio. Some investors with a long-term perspective believe that high volatility is not necessarily bad, because it may well be rewarded by excess return over time. Most investors agree, however, that given two identical sets of returns, they prefer the one that was achieved in the more consistent manner.

In assessing the *ex ante* market volatility of a single portfolio at a specific time, many definitions of beta are possible—weighted actual stock returns over the previous 60 months, up markets versus down markets, exponential weighting to place greater weight on recent time periods, and so on. The beta referred to in this *Handbook*, however, is an *ex post* beta; it pertains to the history of a group of portfolios, not the current holdings.

This *ex post* definition of beta is calculated as the coefficient of a least squares linear regression of composite performance (either monthly or quarterly, as far back as possible) relative to a broad index of market performance (for large-capitalization U.S. equities, usually the S&P 500 Index, but a firm might well justify a different index as more appropriate to its style). A simple regression for such a characteristic line uses absolute returns. A slightly more complicated, but more correct, form was proposed by William F. Sharpe as the capital asset pricing model and adapted by Michael C. Jensen for portfolios. In this case, the equation is defined in terms of excess returns:

$$Y - R_f = \alpha + \beta(X - R_f),$$

where
> Y = firm composite performance
> X = index performance
> α = regression intercept
> β = regression coefficient or slope
> R_f = the risk-free rate of return during the period

The risk-free rate is usually defined as the 90-day U.S. Treasury bill return, but a manager might justifiably use a longer maturity. In either case, the best linear fit of composite performance to the index can be calculated as

$$\beta = \frac{\Sigma(XY)}{\Sigma X^2}$$

and

$$\alpha = \bar{Y} - \beta\bar{X},$$

where $\bar{Y}$ is the average of all months of composite performance (or composite performance in excess of the risk-free rate) and $\bar{X}$ is the average of all months of index performance (or index performance in excess of the risk-free rate).

Sharpe measure. The Sharpe measure, SM_p, is a ratio defined as the excess return earned on a portfolio divided by the volatility of the returns of the securities:

$$SM_p = \frac{(\text{Composite performance} - R_f)}{S_p},$$

where R_f is the risk-free rate of interest and S_p is the standard deviation of the portfolio.

The Sharpe measure is a measure of reward relative to total volatility. An investor might use it, as a framework for looking forward, to help determine the amount of risk required historically to maximize the utility of an investment. A large portfolio of securities should receive some reward for taking on volatility (S_p); otherwise, a portfolio of T-bills would be more sensible than risky securities. As a result, the Sharpe measure, which uses total volatility, seems to be most useful when the portfolio being evaluated represents all of an investor's marketable assets. The Sharpe measure for the portfolio can be compared with the Sharpe measure for the benchmark.

■ *Treynor measure.* The Treynor measure, TM_p, is a ratio defined as the excess return on a portfolio divided by the portfolio's average beta:

$$TM_p = \frac{(\text{Composite performance} - R_f)}{\beta_p}.$$

This ratio is a measure of reward relative to total systematic volatility, or relative risk. The riskiness of individual securities or a small group of securities may best be described by their comovement with the market, β. As a result, the Treynor measure seems to be particularly useful when the investor's portfolio is one of many portfolios included in a large investment fund. The Treynor measure for the portfolio can be compared with the Treynor measure for the benchmark.

The comparison ratios introduced by Sharpe and Treynor have important implications in light of the weaknesses of the primary risk statistics—standard deviation and beta. The bottom line is that no one statistic can consistently capture the riskiness of an asset class or a style of management because of the multifaceted nature of risk. Although not all facets of risk can be captured, the measures described in this section can assist investors in gauging the absolute and relative volatility of an investment strategy or approach by serving as indicators of risk. As long as the shortcomings of these measures are kept clear, each can add valuable insight.

Benchmarks. Benchmarks are used to make risk and return comparisons. As noted in the preceding discussions, the volatility measures are often most valuable when reviewed in relation to one or more benchmarks.

Firms should designate a benchmark and explain its choice. The designated benchmark must be consistently applied and must parallel the risk or investment style the client portfolio is expected to track. For example, a portfolio with 50 percent of its total assets in small-cap to medium-cap stocks and 50 percent in large-cap stocks should be compared with a similarly weighted composite of appropriate indexes rather than a single index. The AIMR-PPS standards recommend disclosure of differences in portfolio structure relative to the designated benchmark.

For multiple-asset composites, firms and clients should agree in advance on the frequency and the assumptions to be used in rebalancing portfolios to the designated benchmark or target allocation.

Benchmarks might be market indexes, manager universes, or

"normal" portfolios. This section explains each type of benchmark and notes its advantages and disadvantages.

Indexes. The most commonly used benchmark for an investment strategy is a market index. Indexes are viewed as "independent representations of the market" and are publicly available. Examples of standardized U.S. market indexes are the S&P 500, Wilshire 5000, and Russell 2000 indexes in the equity market; the Lehman Brothers Government/Corporate or Aggregate, Salomon Brothers Broad Investment Grade, or Merrill Lynch Master indexes in the fixed-income market; and the NCREIF (National Council of Real Estate Investment Fiduciaries) Property Index in the real estate market. In addition to a wide variety of standardized indexes, customized indexes can be created to reflect a specific strategy and universe of securities. Indexes can also be mixed to represent an allocation among markets.

Although indexes are widely used and can offer important insights into relative volatility, the potential for misinterpretation when an index does not accurately reflect the strategy or universe of securities used is significant. In addition, indexes implicitly assume cost-free transactions, and some assume reinvestment of income. Finally, if an index is used as a benchmark, it should be investable, although this characteristic may not be possible for certain indexes.

Manager universes. Consultants and other firms gather data on styles of investment management to create "universes" of return data. These manager performance universes may be valuable for comparative purposes. They have the potential to match portfolio styles more effectively than do indexes, but their use presents some problems in application; for example, different managers may conform to different reporting procedures and different standards of completeness and accuracy of data. Nevertheless, universes remain an important part of measuring relative risk and return.

Normal portfolios. A normal portfolio can be used as a benchmark for investment strategy to provide another kind of measure for evaluating investment decisions. Normal portfolios may offer a valuable means of judging specific risk, for example. Normal portfolios generally suffer from being difficult to construct and maintain, however, and are not generally available from independent sources. They work best when used as a benchmark for a specific client rather than for composite strategy comparison.

In addition to these three types of indexes, a number of other measures have been proposed and used over the years. Anyone judging various approaches to measuring risk should make a more thorough investigation of these techniques and measures than can be presented here. The individual investment strategy should determine the best benchmark or combination of benchmarks. For example, an index strategy must be compared with the appropriate index; a low-P/E fund, because a large population of similar funds and strategies exists and no simple index is available for comparison, may be best judged against an appropriate manager universe. Because active balanced-fund managers may differ substantially in their approaches, the individual risks of such a manager may best be judged against a normal portfolio uniquely defined for that manager.

Composite Dispersion

Composite dispersion measures represent the consistency of a firm's composite performance results with respect to the individual portfolio returns within a composite. The AIMR-PPS standards require that managers disclose the dispersion of portfolio returns within each composite. The appropriate measures of dispersion are (1) for an equal-weighted composite, standard deviation and (2) for an asset-weighted composite, a reformulation of the standard deviation to an asset-weighted dispersion measure or an alternative approach to exhibit consistency. Additional methods are the inclusion of the range of portfolio returns within the composite, high–low portfolio return statistics, and other measures a firm deems valuable.

Standard Deviation. The most widely accepted measure of dispersion within a composite is standard deviation across equal-weighted portfolios, S_c. The definition is as follows:

$$S_c = \sqrt{\frac{\Sigma \, [R_i - MEAN(R)]^2}{n}},$$

where R_i is the return on the ith portfolio, n is the number of portfolios, and $MEAN(R)$ is the equal-weighted mean return, or

$$MEAN(R) = \frac{\Sigma R_i}{n}.$$

Only portfolios that have been managed for the full year should be included in the dispersion calculation, so n in the calculation may be different from the number of portfolios shown in the presentation.

Asset-Weighted Standard Deviation. To create a dispersion measure that explains deviation from the asset-weighted composite is relatively straightforward. The formulation begins with the calculation of an asset-weighted mean. The asset-weighted composite return is formulated as follows:

$$C_{ASSET} = \frac{\Sigma MVB_i(R_i)}{MVB_{TOTAL}},$$

where MVB_i is the market value of the ith portfolio in the composite at the beginning of the period and R_i is the unweighted return on the ith portfolio.

The asset-weighted standard deviation is a better measure of dispersion for an asset-weighted composite because it measures dispersion for the asset-weighted mean composite return. The definition is as follows:

$$S_c = \sqrt{\Sigma W_i\, [R_i - WtMEAN(R)]^2},$$

where W_i is the weight of the ith portfolio in the composite, or MVB_i/MVB_{TOTAL} and $WtMEAN(R)$ is the asset-weighted mean return, or

$$WtMEAN = \frac{\Sigma MVB_i(R_i)}{\Sigma MVB_i}.$$

High–Low and Range. The high–low and range are the simplest and most easily understood measures of dispersion. Their key advantages are simplicity, ease of calculation, and ease of interpretation. On the downside, one extreme value can skew the appearance of the data. In addition, by themselves, the high–low and the range of returns, which will be the same for equal-weighted and asset-weighted composites, are not particularly rigorous. Coupling the high–low and range of returns with other measures, however, such as the quartile dollar dispersion discussed next, increases their value in presentations.

Quartile Dollar Dispersion. High–low and range, by themselves, are not adequate measures of risk because, like standard deviation, they are prone to extreme values that may skew the picture. Therefore, alternative measures of dispersion are helpful. The following example uses the spread of dollars across quartiles to provide additional insights into the dispersion of returns. Note that, even though a portfolio is broken into quartiles, this measure has nothing to do with quartiles for returns shown in manager universes. The data in Table 3 can be used to calculate the rate of return on different quartiles (shown in Table 4). For example, quartile dollar dispersion (QDD) for the worst-performing 25 percent is calculated as

$$QDD4 = \frac{200,000}{250,000}(0.08) + \frac{50,000}{250,000}(0.09).$$

$$= 8.20\%.$$

The rate of return on the best-performing quartile is

$$QDD1 = \frac{100,000}{250,000}(0.15) + \frac{100,000}{250,000}(0.11) + \frac{50,000}{250,000}(0.10).$$

$$= 12.40\%.$$

QDD is not prone to the extremes because it covers one-fourth of the data in both directions. At the same time, it gives investors an idea of the data's dispersion. When it is included with the full high–low range, it may, in fact, give the best idea of dispersion.

Table 3. QDD Example Data

Portfolio	Return	Capitalization
A	8%	$200,000
B	9	200,000
C	10	400,000
D	11	100,000
E	15	100,000

Sample Report and Section Summary. Table 4 provides a sample report showing composite returns and selected risk measures for a year and by quarter. In addition to the data shown in Table 4, the firm has the option of supplementing (not substituting) this table with presentation of equal-weighted data and standard deviations from an equal-weighted mean.

Table 4. Sample Composite Dispersion Report

Period	Asset-Weighted Mean	Highest Performer	QDD1	QDD4	Lowest Performer	Asset-Weighted Dispersion
Year	10.00%	15.00%	12.40%	8.20%	8.00%	1.90%
Q1	4.10	6.00	5.20	3.20	3.00	0.83
Q2	0.50	2.00	1.41	−0.80	−1.00	0.92
Q3	−1.29	0.00	0.24	−2.00	−2.00	0.60
Q4	6.52	8.03	7.78	5.76	5.72	0.88

To summarize, the measures of risk a firm uses should be designed to provide information to clients and potential clients. The best measures have the following properties:

- The measure cannot be manipulated to the firm's advantage.
- The measure is relatively easy to interpret. The mathematical power of a measure matters little unless it can be calculated and interpreted with relative ease.
- The measure applies in a uniform fashion to managers of all sizes.

Leverage

The AIMR-PPS standards require that the use and extent of leverage be disclosed when performance is reported. Firms must disclose the presence of leverage and/or derivatives. The disclosure discussion must contain sufficient detail that current or prospective clients can understand the pattern of returns and the risks from the leverage or derivatives positions.

Multiple-Asset Composite Segments

Firms must disclose whether some or all of the portfolios in a composite are subsectors of larger portfolios and, if so, the percentage of the larger portfolio each subsector represents. Returns of the larger portfolios must be made available.

When the segment returns of multiple-asset portfolios are added to single-asset strategy composites, a cash allocation to each of the segments must be made at the beginning of each reporting period and the cash allocation methodology must be disclosed (see Chapter 2). There is no consensus on a methodology to make the component returns equal to the total return. The AIMR-PPS standards recommend that the return components not be forced to equal the total return, but if a firm chooses to force the components to add up, the firm must disclose the methodology it is using.

Retroactive Compliance

If a firm claims compliance with the AIMR-PPS standards but the firm's pre-January 1, 1993, historical record is not in compliance for all periods and the noncompliance periods are linked to periods that are in compliance, the firm must

- disclose that the full record is not in compliance,
- identify the noncompliance periods, *and*
- explain exactly how the noncompliance periods are out of compliance.

A full discussion regarding retroactive compliance with the AIMR-PPS standards (including a compliance example with effective dates) is provided in the Introduction.

International

The case for reporting international results net of withholding taxes is similar to the case for reporting performance net of transaction costs. Just as a firm's investment performance record includes its ability to negotiate transaction costs, a firm's performance internationally is affected by its ability to choose countries in which to invest based on tax consequences. Country selection is part of the performance process and should include analysis of tax treaties. The impact of specific country taxes should be part of the performance process. Therefore, the percentage of composites for which accrued capital gains taxes on unrealized gains have not been subtracted should be disclosed.

For composites that are defined relative to a benchmark (e.g., portfolios managed against the MSCI Europe/Australia/Far East Index), firms must disclose the percentage of the portfolio invested in countries not contained in the benchmark. The AIMR-PPS standards recommend disclosure of the range or the average country weights in the composite.

Real Estate

Return formulas and accounting policies for items such as capital expenditures, tenant improvements, and leasing commissions must be disclosed. This disclosure must, at a minimum, indicate whether the costs are capitalized or expensed. If costs are capitalized and amortized over some future period(s), this additional information must be included. The required disclosure may appear in the entity's financial statements (usually in the "Significant Accounting Policies" section) and may be incorporated by reference in the AIMR-related disclosures as long as prospective clients have been provided the full financial statements within the last 12 months. In addition, for interim financial statements where full footnote disclosures are not presented, the appropriate disclosures (which would be included in the financial statements in the applicable annual report) may be incorporated by reference as long as prospective clients are provided the most recent annual financial statements.

In order to promote consistent and comparable reporting practices among real estate investment firms that are subject to differing cash distribution and retention policies, firms should include income earned at the investment level in the computation of the income return regardless of the investors' accounting policies for recognizing income from real estate investments.

In addition, questions have arisen about the effects of real estate appraisals on recognizing gains or losses in value in performance periods. Consistent with industry practice, the AIMR-PPS standards require that changes in valuation, including unrealized gains and losses, be recognized in the reporting period that includes the effective date of the appraisal. This requirement is effective for performance presented for periods after December 31, 1993. To clarify: For performance *before* December 1993, either immediate recognition or an allocation of changes in valuation is acceptable, with the disclosure of any change in methodology and the dates affected.

Tax

Most current account and portfolio management systems do not permit managers to extract much of the disclosure information that is necessary to provide meaningful calculation or interpretation of after-tax results. Therefore, after-tax disclosures are currently recommended rather than required. As clients become more sophisticated, the demand for more complete and comparable after-tax reporting information will increase and vendors are likely to develop accounting and portfolio management systems that will meet the types of disclosures recommended.

Wrap Fees

When a firm presents portfolios included in a wrap-fee composite that do not meet the wrap-fee definition, the firm must disclose for each year presented (1) the dollar amount of assets represented and (2) the fee deducted.

If a wrap-fee composite is presented to non-wrap-fee clients, the firm must present a description of the fee and investment style and must disclose that gross-of-fees returns may not include transaction costs.

5. Verification

The AIMR-PPS standards recommend that firms verify their claims that performance is in compliance with the Standards. If a firm undertakes verification, the verification must be performed by an independent third party. Verification consists of two levels: Level I verification applies to all firm composites; Level II verification applies to specific composites and requires a Level I verification at least of the specific composites being verified at Level II.

When a verification statement is issued, the verifier *must* include in the attestation statement whether a Level I or Level II verification was performed. This statement must be made either in the text of the report or in a footnote (see Exhibit 3). *Without such a statement from the verifier, the firm cannot claim that its investment performance has been verified.*

Recommendations

1. Level I Verification

   This level requires:

   - independent attestation that the requirements of the AIMR-PPS standards have been met on a firmwide basis,
   - that each of the firm's discretionary fee-paying portfolios is included in at least one composite and that the firm's procedures for assigning portfolios to composites are reasonable and have been consistently applied over time, *and*
   - examination of the firm's procedures for calculating total, time-weighted returns, taking into account lost accounts, making appropriate disclosures, and presenting results.

2. Level II Verification

   This level requires that:

   - Level I verification has been performed (at least) on the specific composites being verified at Level II,
   - performance results of specific composites have been calculated according to the AIMR-PPS standards, *and*
   - composites include only appropriate, actual discretionary fee-paying portfolios and do not exclude any other portfolios meeting the same criteria representing a similar strategy or investment objective.

Exhibit 3. Example Verification Statement

The example's language is subject to any applicable professional standards of the verifier:

Level I: Verifier [X, name of verifier] has completed a Level I verification of compliance in accordance with the AIMR Performance Presentation Standards (AIMR-PPS™) for Firm [XYZ, name of firm] for the time period [time period]. In the opinion of Verifier [X], the requirements of the AIMR Performance Presentation Standards have been met on a firmwide basis.

Level II: Verifier [X, name of verifier] has completed a Level II verification of compliance in accordance with the AIMR Performance Presentation Standards (AIMR-PPS™) on Composite [A, identification of composite] for Firm [XYZ, name of firm] for the time period [time period]. In the opinion of Verifier [X], Composite [A]: (1) includes all of the firm's actual discretionary fee-paying portfolios that share the similar strategy or investment objective in the firm's definition of this composite and (2) includes composite securities, income, and pricing data that are valid; (3) performance results have been calculated in compliance with the AIMR-PPS standards.

Firm [XYZ] has represented to Verifier [X] in writing: (1) that Firm [XYZ] complies with the AIMR-PPS standards on a firmwide basis and (2) that a list of all firm composites is available and the required disclosures for each composite have been made.

Verifier [X] is not responsible for the accuracy of the list of firm composites and has relied solely upon information provided by Firm [XYZ] for its claim of firmwide compliance with the AIMR-PPS standards.

In order to claim compliance with the AIMR-PPS standards, compliance must be *firmwide*. Claims of product or composite compliance are not permitted. All requirements and disclosures of the Standards must be met for *all* actual discretionary fee-paying portfolios of the firm. Level II *verification* may be composite specific, but compliance with the AIMR-PPS standards must be firmwide.

The following verification procedures are minimum procedures that must be followed when a verification of compliance with the AIMR-PPS standards is conducted and a statement of verification is issued. These procedures are intended to standardize verification. Verification engagements may involve situations that prevent a step from being followed or cause a step to be not applicable, however; in such a situation, alteration of the procedures, when significant, must be disclosed in the verification statement.

Preverification Procedures

Knowledge of the Business. Verifiers must obtain the firm's most recent investment performance reports and other available financial data for the firm, including the firm's most recent Form ADV or brochure. Verifiers must also review published articles, if any, that relate to the firm or to the investment manager and review and discuss the performance data with appropriate firm personnel to gain understanding of the types of investment strategies offered, types of clients served, scope of business, and volume of assets under management.

Verifiers must understand the requirements and recommendations of the AIMR-PPS standards as published in the *AIMR Performance Presentation Standards Handbook* second edition and any other updates, reports, or clarifications published by AIMR.

Verifiers who are Certified Public Accountants must read and understand the Statement on Standards for Attestation Engagement.

Knowledge of the Standards Used by the Firm for Performance Presentation. Through discussions with appropriate firm personnel, verifiers must determine the assumptions and policies in place at the firm for the following items and disclose any differences between firm standards and the AIMR-PPS standards:

- policy with regard to investment discretion; the verifier must receive from the firm, in writing, the firm's definition of investment discretion and the firm's guidelines for determining whether accounts are fully discretionary in the investment sense;
- policy with regard to the definition of composites according to investment strategy; the verifier must obtain the firm's list of composite definitions with written criteria for including accounts in one composite versus another;
- policy with regard to the timing of inclusion of new accounts in the composites;
- policy with regard to timing of exclusion of closed accounts in the composites;
- policy with regard to the accrual of interest and dividend income;
- policy with regard to the market valuation of investment securities (including use of trade- or settlement-date accounting);
- method for computing time-weighted portfolio return;
- policy with regard to the calculation of total return;
- assumptions on the timing of capital inflows/outflows;

- method for computing the composite's average return;
- policy with regard to the portability of portfolio results;
- policy with regard to the presentation of composites and annual returns;
- method of cash allocation for inclusion of balanced composite assets in a single-asset composite;
- policies regarding timing of implied taxes due on income and realized capital gains for after-tax performance;
- policies regarding use of securities/countries not included in the composite's benchmark for international performance;
- any other policies and procedures relevant to performance presentation.

Level I Verification

A Level I verification attests that the requirements of the AIMR-PPS standards have been met on a firmwide basis. For example, the verifier must attest that the following requirements have been met:
- All of the firm's actual discretionary fee-paying portfolios are included in appropriate composites defined according to investment strategy or investment objective.
- A full listing of composites is available.
- Portfolio returns are calculated according to a time-weighted return methodology with a minimum of quarterly valuation and accrual of income for fixed-income securities.
- Portfolio returns within the composites are weighted by beginning-of-period asset value.
- The performance presentation for each composite includes the number of portfolios in the composite, the amount of composite assets, composite assets as a percentage of total firm assets, and a measure of annual dispersion. This information must be available on at least an annual basis for each year for which compliance with the AIMR-PPS standards is claimed.
- Disclosures have been provided to ensure that performance has been presented accurately and in keeping with the full and fair presentation of investment results.

Accrual accounting for equities is not required but is recommended, particularly if cash-basis accounting distorts performance reporting.

Account Inclusion/Exclusion. Verifiers look at the firm's policies on the inclusion and exclusion of portfolios in composites to determine that

- the manager's definition of discretion has been consistently applied over time;
- the firm has defined composites according to reasonable guidelines that have been consistently applied over time;
- all actual discretionary fee-paying portfolios have been included in at least one composite and the portfolios have been grouped according to consistently applied composite definitions;
- all discretionary fee-paying portfolios no longer under management have been included in appropriate composites up to the last full valuation period under management;
- all new actual discretionary fee-paying portfolios have been added to the appropriate composite after the portfolio has been under management for one full valuation period or according to guidelines that have been consistently applied and are appropriate to the composite's investment strategy;
- shifts of portfolios from one composite to another have been based on documented changes in client guidelines and the criteria for shifts in composites have been consistently applied.

Verification Procedures. Verifiers must adhere to the following procedures:

1. Obtain a listing of open and closed accounts for all composites for the years under examination and perform the following:
   - For selected accounts (see following section for selection process) opened in the year of examination, determine whether the timing of the initial inclusion in the composite is in accordance with policies of the firm.
   - For selected accounts closed in the year of examination, determine whether the timing of exclusion from the composite is in accordance with policies of the firm.

2. For each selected account:
   - Determine, by reference to the account agreement and the manager's written guidelines for determining investment discretion, whether the manager's classification of the account as discretionary or nondiscretionary is appropriate.
   - Determine, by reference to the account agreement, portfolio summary, and the manager's list of composite definitions, whether the objectives set forth in the account agreement are consistent with the manager's composite definition for that account.

3. Using appropriate sampling:

   - Trace selected accounts from account agreements to the master account listing.
   - Trace selected accounts from the master account listing to the yearly composites covering the years under examination.

4. Using the guidelines set forth by the U.S. Securities and Exchange Commission staff concerning performance reporting gross or net of fees:

   - Determine whether the client firm is permitted to disclose results gross or net of advisory fees.
   - Determine whether a change has occurred in the firm's organizational structure that might cause a significant alteration of composite results.

5. Ensure the following for all composites:

   - All portfolios sharing the same guidelines are included in the same composite and shifts from one composite to another are consistent with the guidelines set forth by the specific "adjusted" account agreement or with documented guidelines of the firm's clients.
   - Portfolio returns within the composite are weighted by size.
   - Performance is calculated using a time-weighted rate of return, with a minimum of quarterly valuations and accrual of income for fixed-income securities. (Accrual accounting for equities is not required but is recommended, particularly if cash-basis accounting distorts performance reporting.)
   - Disclosures are offered to ensure that performance has been presented accurately and in keeping with a full and fair presentation.

6. Verify completeness of the managed accounts included in the firm's list of composites by selecting and examining a sample composite (see the next section).

   ▨ *Sample selection and examination.* The verifier's selection criteria should take the following items into consideration:
   - environmental aspects (business, politics, socioeconomics, social, etc.),
   - number of composites at the firm,
   - number of portfolios in each composite,

- nature of the composite,
- total assets under management,
- internal control structure at the firm (system of checks and balances in place),
- number of years under examination,
- risk and materiality (see the following section on risk and materiality),
- computer applications, software in use in the construction of composites, and the calculation of performance results,
- client firm's commitment to fair presentation of performance under the AIMR-PPS standards, and
- intended use and distribution of the verification report.

This list is not all-inclusive; the items are the minimum requirements that should be used in the selection and evaluation of a sample for testing. For example, choosing a portfolio for the study sample that has the largest impact on composite performance because of its size or because of extremely good or bad performance may be useful.

Based on these criteria, verifiers must make sample selections (two different samples may have to be used for Level I and Level II verifications). This sample is referred to as the "basic sample" and will be used for most of the detailed testing.

A relatively small sample of data may satisfy the verifier that appropriate procedures and computer software are in place to calculate performance correctly. The lack of explicit audit trails or the presence of apparent errors may warrant selecting a larger sample or applying additional verification procedures. The verifier may conclude that some performance records do not lend themselves to a complete verification. In such a case, the verifier must issue a qualified verification report clarifying why a completely satisfactory opinion was not possible.

▓ *Risk and materiality.* Verifiers must assess the risk associated with the particular engagement and evaluate the internal controls at the client firm. Based on this evaluation, verifiers must develop guidelines as to whether the effects of the errors and qualitative information would be material. The initial assessment may have to be revised should new relevant information be uncovered during the verification.

Level II Verification

When issuing a Level II verification on a specific composite, a verifier must perform at least an abbreviated Level I verification. This verification will consist of a determination by the verifier that

- the composite involved in the Level II verification is constructed in accordance with the AIMR-PPS standards,
- all of the firm's other actual discretionary fee-paying portfolios are included in a composite, and
- at all times, all accounts belong in their respective composites and no accounts that belong in a particular composite have been excluded.

Level II verification must be accompanied by a firmwide list of composites and the required disclosures for each composite (e.g., number of portfolios, composite assets, and the composite assets as a percentage of firm assets). Without the list of firmwide composites, the firm cannot claim a Level II verification. The firm is obligated to attach the composite list to the Level II verification statement.

Verifiers must

- understand the appropriateness and calculation basis of benchmarks included in performance statistics for comparison and
- understand the appropriateness and calculation of risk statistics included in performance statistics for comparison.

■ *Cash flows, income, and expenses.* Verifiers must determine whether capital contributions and withdrawals that are used in the performance calculations are recorded in the proper accounts, at the right amounts, and on a timely basis. Verifiers should carry out the following procedures:

1. For each account in the selected sample basis, verify income streams, including the timing and actual receipt of dividends, accrued interest, other income, and treatment of various fees and expenses. Dividends may be recorded on a cash basis, but AIMR recommends accrual-basis treatment.

2. Agree dividend payments to an independent source on a test basis.

3. Recalculate interest income and various fees and agree to custodian statement on a test basis.

4. Trace cash flows to appropriate independent documentation and ensure bona fide recording in the proper account and proper period.

5. Footnote cash flow details on the transaction detail report for a number of individual accounts on a test basis.

6. Obtain and review bank reconciliation to ensure proper recording of cash flows.

7. Agree to composite schedule.

8. Determine the reasonableness of the methods used to account for cash flows of managed accounts.

    ▨ *Portfolio trade processing.* Verifiers must determine whether executed trades have been recorded in the proper accounts at the correct amounts on the appropriate dates. Verifiers should carry out the following procedures:

1. For each composite or custodian statement, trace the trade to the following:

    • agree the CUSIP (Committee on Uniform Securities Identification Procedures) number, equity name, trade date, settlement date, price per share (principal amount), and total cost of proceeds on the transaction summary principal cash ledger to the custodian statement;

    • agree the CUSIP number, equity name, trade date, settlement date, price per share (principal amount), and total cost of proceeds on the transaction summary principal cash ledger to the independent broker confirmation;

    • ascertain the reasonableness of the purchase/sales price of a security from an independent pricing source;

    • trace each purchase/sale selection to the daily listing of portfolios and ensure proper inclusion/exclusion;

    • verify distributions based on the allocation sheet showing the breakup and distribution of total purchase/sale to various customer accounts, if applicable;

    • agree exchange rates to independent source, if applicable.

2. Agree to composite schedule.

    ▨ *Portfolio valuation management.* Verifiers must determine whether the end-of-month (quarter) valuation of the security positions is accurate. Verifiers should carry out the following procedures:

1. For each account selected in the basic sample, obtain the client firm's end-of-month (quarter) portfolio price makeup sheet and perform the following:

    • agree all securities on the price makeup sheet to the month-end custodian statement (exceptions may arise because of unsettled purchases/sales transactions and differences in security prices);

- agree open purchases/sales to the subsequent custodian statement for clearance, if applicable;
- agree the market value of the price makeup sheet to an independent price source on a test basis;
- on a test basis, recalculate and footnote the total market valuation from the summary position sheet and agree to the list performance detail report,
- agree exchange rates to an independent source, if applicable.

2. Agree to composite schedule.

3. Obtain externally pooled portfolio records (custodian statements) or historical internally produced documents (customer statements) and agree to portfolio valuation in the composite, as applicable and practicable.

   Performance measurement calculation. Verifiers must

- determine whether the client firm's performance measurement statistics have been computed in accordance with the AIMR-PPS standards;
- determine whether the client firm's performance measurement statistics have been computed in accordance with the policies and assumptions indicated by the firm in the footnotes to the report.

For these tasks, verifiers should carry out the following procedures:

1. Obtain from the client firm the composite schedule for composite accounts for the years under examination; recalculate quarterly (monthly) rates of return for each account in the basic sample using an acceptable return formula as prescribed by AIMR (i.e., time-weighted rate of return) based on the information contained in the composites.

2. Recalculate the following for all composites under examination and agree to the client firm's reported figures:
   - the linked annual rates of return for all composite accounts under examination;
   - the average annual rate of return for all composites under examination.

3. Agree composite schedule to cash flows, trade tickets, and portfolio positions tested previously.

■ *Net-of-fees testing.* When a manager chooses to create and verify net-of-fees performance results, the verifier must determine whether the calculation of the net-of-fees performance is accurate. Verifiers should carry out the following procedures:

1. Obtain quarterly (monthly) customer invoices for each selected portfolio.

2. Recompute the fee per the invoice and agree the total quarterly fee to the sum of the related monthly fees or the performance detail report.

3. Recalculate the monthly allocation, which is based on the portfolio market value weighted by each month (for billings in arrears) or by dividing the quarterly fee by 3 (for billings in advance). For any discrepancies, agree allocation used to the client firm's fee schedule. (Recalculate fees based on the client firm's contracts on a test basis.)

4. Test allocations of fees to specific managed accounts; consider impact of allocation methodology on time-weighted performance calculations.

5. Agree the fees per the performance detail report to the fees listed per the related composite performance report.

All Verifications

Verifiers have responsibilities in the areas of report reviews and maintaining documents to support the verifier's conclusions:

1. Verifiers must read the performance report footnotes and determine whether they are complete and accurate based on knowledge of the client firm's performance calculations and the disclosure requirements for examinations performed in accordance with the AIMR-PPS standards.

2. The verifier must independently verify every disclosure, statement, and amount. The verifier must maintain adequate work papers to support the disclosed data.

3. The verifier must obtain a representation letter from the client firm confirming major policies and any other specific representations made to the verifier during the examination, including that the firm complies with the AIMR-PPS standards on a firm-wide basis.

Appendix A. Sample Composite Returns Format and Supplemental Information

Returns Format

Return	1Q 199x	2Q 199x	3Q 199x	4Q 199x
Before-tax return				
Client's after-tax return				
Firm's adjusted after-tax return				

Supplemental Information

Category	1Q 199x	2Q 199x	3Q 199x	4Q 199x
Beginning market value				
Ending market value				
Percentage taxable securities (ending)				
Percentage tax-exempt securities (ending)				
Contributions				
Withdrawals				
Beginning unrealized gains				
Ending unrealized gains				
Realized short-term capital gains[a]				
Realized long-term capital gains[a]				
Taxable income				
Treasury income				
Taxable state income				
Tax-exempt income				
Number of portfolios				
Composite assets				
Composite assets as a percentage of firm assets				
Composite assets as a percentage of taxable assets managed according to same strategy				

[a]Footnote to disclose the accounting convention for treatment of realized capital gains—highest cost, average cost, lowest cost, FIFO, LIFO, etc.

Appendix B. Examples of Performance Presentation Involving Leverage

This appendix sets forth several examples, with comments and recommended treatment for performance presentation, of the procedures recommended in the AIMR-PPS standards for dealing with portfolios using leverage and/or derivatives. In this discussion, two universally accepted definitions of leverage in the investment context—the accounting definition and the economic definition—are used. One definition may be more appropriate than the other in a specific case. An *accountant* would say that leverage results when total assets are greater than net assets—that is, when some part of the assets is financed by liabilities, or borrowing. An *economist* (or perhaps a portfolio manager) would say that leverage results when supplementary investment actions are taken to generate returns from an unleveraged benchmark portfolio.

The following examples pertain to the presentation of composite performance to prospective clients. The treatments are the same for current clients, but in that case, the presentation of supplemental information is recommended rather than required.

Example 1: A firm is given a portfolio of $100 million, with the discretion to increase exposure to the market by buying S&P 500 Index futures worth 50 percent of the underlying assets. The firm chooses to increase market exposure by 20 percent.

> *Treatment*: Because the firm has discretion to increase exposure to the stock market, performance should reflect the firm's decisions of whether to increase exposure and by how much. Performance presented must be on the underlying assets of $100 million. In addition, the all-cash return must be calculated on the leveraged base of $120 million and must be provided as supplemental information. The firm would include $100 million in total firm assets and report an additional $50 million in a separate category of leveraged assets (even though the manager has chosen to leverage by only $20 million).

Example 2: A firm is given a portfolio of $100 million with directions from the client to increase exposure to the market by buying S&P 500 futures equal to 50 percent of the underlying assets.

Treatment: Because the firm does not have discretion over the amount of leverage, the all-cash return must be calculated on a base of $150 million; this return may be included in the same composite with other unleveraged S&P 500 portfolios. Total firm assets include $150 million.

Example 3: A firm is given a portfolio of $1 million. The client borrows $250,000 from the broker against the portfolio.

Treatment: Performance is based on $1 million, and this amount is included in total firm assets.

Example 4: A firm is given a portfolio of $1 million with discretion to leverage the account via margin by 50 percent. The firm margins the account up to $1.25 million.

Treatment: Performance must be shown on a leveraged basis, using $1 million as the base. In addition, performance must be shown as supplemental information on an all-cash basis using $1.25 million as the base. Total assets under management are $1 million, with an additional $0.5 million of margined assets.

Example 5: A firm is given a portfolio of $100 million and instructed by the client to overlay the portfolio with a tactical asset allocation strategy up to 50 percent of the portfolio's market value.

Treatment: The leveraged return calculated on a base of $100 million must be shown, with the all cash return on the amount of underlying assets plus actual leveraged assets shown as supplemental information. The amount of assets included in total firm assets is $100 million. The additional $50 million of potential overlay assets is reported separately in an overlay assets category.

Example 6: A firm is contracted to overlay a $100 million portfolio with a tactical asset allocation strategy equal to 50 percent of the underlying assets. The firm does not manage the underlying assets.

Treatment: Performance of the overlay strategy is based on $50 million, which should always be the actual amount invested in the strategy. No assets are included in total firm assets because the firm does not manage the underlying securities. The $50 million is reported in a separate overlay assets category.

Example 7: A firm is contracted to overlay a $100 million portfolio with a tactical asset allocation strategy up to 50 percent of the underlying assets. The firm does not manage the underlying assets.

Treatment: Performance of the overlay strategy is based on the actual amount of assets invested in the overlay strategy. Performance based on the potential $50 million in overlay assets must also be shown as supplemental information. No assets are included in total firm assets because the firm does not manage the underlying assets. The full $50 million is reported in a separate overlay assets category.

The following scenarios illustrate that leverage can occur without derivatives through margin buying or short selling and that derivatives need not give rise to leverage or necessitate restating to an all-cash basis. In each case, the firms do not have discretion over the amount or timing of the leverage.

Example 8: A firm is given $5,000 to invest in securities on behalf of an account. The firm purchases $10,000 in stocks on margin. This portfolio is leveraged in both the accounting and economic senses. The $10,000 purchase exceeds the $5,000 investment because of the borrowing of $5,000 for margin. Also, the portfolio must achieve roughly twice the return of a portfolio for which the manager held $5,000 in the same stocks without borrowing (adjusted for borrowing cost).

> *Comment:* Few people would dispute that leverage has been used in this example. Moreover, the restatement to an all-cash basis is fairly straightforward and will use the actual accounting records for the transactions involved (purchase of stock, borrowing of margin, payment of margin interest, etc.). This restatement goes to all cash by recasting the portfolio to appear as though it were $10,000 rather than $5,000.

> *Recommendation:* Disclosure of the portfolio as being leveraged is required, and any additional information about the use of leverage must be thoroughly discussed. The all-cash return must be computed and disclosed.

Example 9: A firm purchases $10 million in an S&P index fund and buys $10 million in S&P 500 stock index futures for an account.

> *Comment:* This portfolio must be viewed as leveraged, as opposed to being considered an equity portfolio with a beta of 2.0. Any restatement of the return to an all-cash basis would recast the portfolio as though it were $20 million. The principle that requires all-cash restatement for this portfolio is that one could obtain the same leverage by borrowing $10 million and buying

the stocks, making the portfolio look like the portfolio in Example 8. Because the portfolio in Example 8 can and must be restated to an all-cash basis, the portfolio in Example 9 must likewise be restated.

Consider what it would mean to calculate the incremental return as the difference between the total fund return and the fund return without derivatives. This equity portfolio is most likely managed with the objective of being a competitive equity portfolio in its own right. The futures are probably not part of the equity management strategy itself but, instead, are probably intended to meet other strategic objectives, such as asset allocation, market timing, or hedging other assets not in the portfolio. Thus, without further disclosure of the purpose of the futures, calculating the incremental return would probably be neither meaningful nor representative because of the use of the futures.

Recommendation: Disclosure of the portfolio as being leveraged is required, with whatever additional information about the use of the futures and leverage thoroughly discussed. The all-cash return must be computed and disclosed. Because futures prices incorporate imputed borrowing costs, the method of computing the all-cash return is consistent with that proposed for the portfolio in Example 8. The all-cash return would be the ending total portfolio value, including the ending futures value, divided by $20 million.

Example 10: A firm has used an account's total assets of $5,000 to buy call options on stocks ($5,000 is the premium cost, not the underlying value of the calls). This portfolio is not leveraged in an accounting sense, because the total assets and net assets are equal at $5,000, with no liability or borrowing in the portfolio. The portfolio is clearly leveraged in an economic sense, however, because the returns will be proportionately much different from a portfolio that bought the stocks instead of the calls on the stocks.

Comment: The portfolio in Example 10 may or may not be considered leveraged. If considered leveraged, it could be argued that it is already on an all-cash basis because no borrowing has occurred; the calls were purchased for cash. If there were to be any restatement, it would probably be to reflect the returns from a portfolio of the underlying stocks purchased for cash. Such a restatement would be forced to rely on hypothetical transactions involving the assumed prices at which the stocks could have been purchased, commissions, and so forth. The firm must disclose the strategy used, the risk–return profile of the strategy, and the impact on portfolio return.

Recommendation: Although this strategy might not be called leveraged, disclosure of the portfolio strategy used is required. The principle that requires disclosure is in the spirit of the requirement pertaining to the leverage—that the portfolio may experience unusual levels of risk or return because of the nature of the strategy used. The returns need not be restated on an all-cash basis, because the portfolio is already truly all cash and any restatement to the comparable stock portfolio would rely on hypothetical transactions. Restatements that are not verifiable or do not rely on actual transactions must be avoided.

Example 11: A firm holds $8,000 in stocks on margin and has sold $3,000 worth of stock index futures for an account with a net worth of $5,000. This portfolio is leveraged in an accounting sense in the same way as Example 8. It is not leveraged in an economic sense because the futures hedge $3,000 of the stocks and the remaining $5,000 in stocks will then produce returns roughly equal to a portfolio that held $5,000 in the same stocks without borrowing.

Comment: As in Example 10, this portfolio may or may not be considered leveraged. If leveraged, restatement to an all-cash basis could take two forms. First, the restatement could remove the gain or loss on the short futures (working from actual accounting records) and then proceed as in Example 8. The philosophy of this method is that the stocks, when viewed in the absence of the futures, are leveraged and must be restated accordingly. Second, the restatement could remove the gain or loss on the futures and adjust the stock portfolio (by using prices, commissions, etc.). Unlike the first method, this restatement goes to all cash by "unwinding" the margin transaction back to a $5,000 portfolio size. The philosophy of this method is that the sale of the futures was done as an alternative to actually selling $3,000 of stocks and had the stocks been sold, there would have been no leverage. The manager must disclose the strategy used, the risk–return profile of the strategy, and the impact on portfolio return.

Recommendation: Disclosure of the portfolio strategy used is recommended but not required. The portfolio, as given, is not leveraged relative to a fully invested, unleveraged stock portfolio and must not be expected to have unusual levels of risk or return. If the portfolio may use actual leverage on occasion, however, or if the futures hedge is an active timing decision, then disclosure of the portfolio strategy used is required. In the former case, restatement to an all-cash basis is not needed. In the latter case, restatement may be recommended, depending on the actual strategy used, whether the strategy could actually be executed on an all-cash basis, and whether restatement based solely on actual transactions is possible.

Example 12: A firm has sold short $1,000 in stocks and bought $1,000 in other stocks for an account with a net worth of $5,000. This portfolio is leveraged in an accounting sense because selling short creates a liability to buy back the short stock and because total assets of $6,000 are greater than the net assets of $5,000. This portfolio is not leveraged in the strictest economic sense because the portfolio may not produce a return much different from a portfolio of $5,000 in cash equivalents (assuming the long and short stocks are reasonably well correlated with each other and hedge each other).

> *Comment:* The portfolio in Example 12 may not be leveraged according to the strict economic definition, but it is certainly leveraged on the basis of other investment considerations. The portfolio return clearly depends on the returns of the long versus short stocks. Moreover, the portfolio achieves this return without any outlay of cash (assuming the technical details of the use of proceeds from short sales is ignored). Because the portfolio could have been long and short $5,000 in stocks just as easily as $1,000, clearly the return between the long and short stocks can be (or already is being) leveraged. This portfolio would not be restated to an all-cash position because what "all cash" means with regard to short sales is not clear. The firm must disclose the strategy used, the risk–return profile of the strategy, and the impact of the strategy on portfolio return.

> *Recommendation:* Disclosure of the portfolio strategy used is required because the portfolio may experience unusual levels of risk or return as a result of the strategy. The returns need not be restated to an all-cash basis because the strategy cannot be executed without short sales, which makes the term "all cash" meaningless.

Example 13: Firm A has four clients for which securities are traded. Firm A prefers to have the clients trade on margin because of the greater leverage, but two clients do not permit trading on margin. Firm A has received $30,000 from each of the two clients who do not permit trading on margin and $15,000 from each of the two clients who do permit trading on margin. Firm A will trade all four accounts the same; that is, the same securities will be purchased or sold in the same quantities at the same time for each account. In the first month, Firm A makes $50 in profit for each account.

Firm B is a futures trader and accepts an $800,000 account from a client who deposits $200,000 for margin. Firm B has one other client, who also has allocated $800,000, and this client has all $800,000 deposited in the account. The trading for each account is identical. In the first month, Firm B earns $5,000 in profit for each client.

> *Comment*: This example illustrates a situation in which a firm trades some accounts within a composite at different levels of leverage. If the strategies for the portfolios are the same, they must be included in the same composite. To avoid performance distortion, the firms must restate the leveraged returns to an all-cash basis. Firm A must disclose the two accounts on margin and restate them to an all-cash basis as in Example 8. For Firm B, restatement requires that the returns be calculated on the basis of the amount of assets allocated to the firm for investment (as opposed to only the amount deposited into the account for margin). Without restatement, composite results are distorted because of the "blended return" from portfolios trading at different levels of leverage.
>
> At the end of the first month, Firm A and Firm B have earned the following returns on a blended basis:
>
> Firm A: $\dfrac{\$200}{\$90,000} = 0.22\%$
>
> and
>
> Firm B: $\dfrac{\$10,000}{\$1,000,000} = 1.00\%.$
>
> On an all-cash basis,
>
> Firm A: $\dfrac{\$200}{\$120,000} = 0.17\%$
>
> and
>
> Firm B: $\dfrac{\$10,000}{\$1,600,000} = 0.63\%.$

Recommendation: For Firm A, disclosure of the two accounts as leveraged is required, with whatever additional information about the use of leverage thoroughly discussed. The all-cash restatement must be computed and disclosed for the same reasons discussed in Example 8, as well as to avoid the reporting of "blended" returns. For Firm B, disclosure of the strategy used is required, especially with respect to the client who has deposited only margin funds, because the portfolios may experience unusual levels of risk or return as a result of the strategy used. Returns for the client who has deposited only margin funds need to be restated using the amount of assets allocated to the firm, which must be disclosed. This allocation must be verifiable on the basis of the client agreement with the firm.

Example 14: A firm is managing a market-neutral strategy using phantom cash. In this case, the term "phantom cash" refers to the aggregate amount of cash that a client might have with multiple firms, with responsibility for managing the cash placed with one firm in particular. The firm is allowed to leverage the cash position by a multiple of 2.5 times.

Comment: The portfolio is not leveraged in a strict economic sense because the return may not differ from a portfolio of cash equivalents, assuming that the long and short securities are reasonably well correlated with each other and hedge each other to produce a market-neutral strategy. It is leveraged in some sense, however, because the portfolio's return clearly depends on the returns of the long versus short securities and because the strategy can be used without any outlay of cash (ignoring the technical details of the use of proceeds from the short sales).

Recommendation: The firm must disclose the risk–return profile of the strategy and its potential impact on portfolio return. Because what "all cash" means with regard to short sales is unclear, the portfolio would not be restated to an all-cash position. To illustrate, assume that a client allocates $10 million in cash to a firm that will then leverage this cash position by 2.5 times. The firm will go long $25 million in one type of security and go short $25 million in other securities. The cash may not be in an account that is directly attributable to the firm—that is, the client may be allocating cash that is actually held in accounts being managed by multiple firms—but one firm is assigned the management of a total amount of cash earmarked for a market-neutral strategy. The returns to the market-neutral strategy would be based on $10 million, with disclosure of the type of strategy being used. Restatement to an all-cash basis would not be possible. The $25 million would be reported separately as part of cash overlay assets; $10 million would be included in firm assets.

When presenting performance of derivative strategies for portfolios consisting primarily of other types of assets, the incremental returns must be calculated by taking the difference between the total fund return and the return on the fund without the contribution of the derivative securities. The methodology used to do this must be disclosed and consistently applied, and it must be based on actual transactions and their accounting records. The following three examples illustrate the issues in calculating performance for derivative strategies.

Example 15: This portfolio uses an option-overwriting strategy whereby stocks are managed by one portfolio manager with the objective of producing competitive equity portfolio returns while a second portfolio manager (within the same firm) writes covered call options on the stocks with the objective of adding incremental income to the portfolio. (This kind of overwriting strategy usually involves identification of stocks with little potential for much upside in the near term—but with good long-term potential—and normally uses out-of-the-money calls.)

> *Comment*: In Example 15, the equity portfolio is managed to be a competitive equity portfolio in its own right. The overwriting of call options is clearly intended to produce incremental return. Up to this point, the calculation and reporting of the return without the calls and the incremental return from the derivatives (i.e., calls) seems useful. But there is one major problem. When a call is exercised, the portfolio is obligated to deliver the stock or, in effect, sell the stock at the strike price of the call. The exercise of a call results in the portfolio selling a stock at a price at which it might not otherwise have been sold. For example, if a call gets exercised at a strike price of $35, the equity manager will be unable to sell at her intended price target of something higher, say, $39. Thus, the return on the portfolio without the contribution of the calls does not actually measure what the equity manager would have done without the derivatives.

Recommendation: If this portfolio is included in an equity compos-ite, disclosure of the portfolio strategy is required because the covered-call writing may have significant effects vis-á-vis an equi-ty portfolio. The performance of the equity portfolio in the absence of the derivatives strategy cannot be accurately determined with-out the use of hypothetical transactions, as discussed previously. Thus, calculation of the returns on the total fund without the derivatives or the incremental return is not recommended.

Example 16: A portfolio uses a buy-and-write strategy whereby stocks are purchased and covered call options are simultaneously written on the stocks. The manager's objective is to produce returns a few percentage points above cash-equivalent yields with low risk of negative returns. (This kind of buy-and-write strategy usually involves identifying stocks with little downside risk and normally uses in-the-money calls.)

Comment: Example 16 appears similar to Example 15, with both portfolios buying stocks and selling calls. In fact, it may be difficult to distinguish between the two by looking at a list of portfolio holdings. The role of the options in each case, however, is different. In Example 16, the written call is intended to act more as a price hedge and, when coupled with the stock, to behave as a cash equivalent. In Example 15, the written call is not explicitly intended to be a price hedge but to produce incremental income. The role of the stocks is also different in the two examples. In Example 15, the stocks are chosen on their merits as an equity investment. In Example 16, a stock and written call act as a hedged unit that cannot be considered separately in a meaningful way.

A further complication in Example 16 is that trade orders for buy-and-write's may be placed on a net basis, such as "buy the stock and sell the call for a net debit of $17." This order may be filled either by buying the stock at $20 and selling the call at $3 or by buying the stock at $20.25 and selling the call at $3.25; either way will net a cost of $17 and the effect on the total portfolio and its return is the same. But the calculation of returns without the contribution of derivatives would be affected be-cause whether the stock costs $20.00 or $20.25 is important to the equity-only return. Thus, for Example 16, the calculation and reporting of the return without the calls and the incremental return is not appropriate.

Recommendation: It is recommended that the portfolio not be included in an equity composite because this particular portfolio has characteristics akin to cash management. If the portfolio is included in a cash-management composite, disclosure of the portfolio strategy is required because the returns will likely be significantly different from ordinary cash-management returns. Because of the nature of the buy-and-write strategy, calculation of returns on the total fund without the derivatives or the incremental return is not meaningful and, hence, is not recommended.

Example 17: The portfolio is an enhanced index fund that uses derivatives to add incremental value above the S&P 500 with little risk of underperforming. For example, the portfolio may sell a basket of S&P 500 stocks and replace them with T-bills (or other cash equivalents) and S&P stock index futures.

Comment: A typical use of derivatives in Example 17 would involve selling stocks and simultaneously buying S&P 500 futures in an equal amount. Such trades are often done on the basis of the relative prices between the stocks and futures—that is, when the futures are inexpensive relative to the stocks net of all transaction costs. The practical result of such trades is that the stock portfolio absorbs some transaction costs, which creates a drag on the total stock performance but is more than offset by incremental gains in the futures position. A further complication is that such trades are often done as principal trades when a net valuation spread between the stocks is above or below the current quoted market. Again, this stock mispricing is more than offset in the futures pricing via the pricing of the net trade. Thus, the return on the portfolio without the contribution of the derivatives (i.e., the stock portfolio return) is actually influenced by the derivatives strategy, as in Example 16. These effects on returns may be small, but they are definitely significant; the stock portfolio is an index fund, and a few basis points of "noise" in the return can represent significant and noticeable tracking error in a highly competitive index fund market.

Recommendation: If the portfolio is included in an equity composite, disclosure of the portfolio strategy is required because the returns may be significantly affected by the derivatives. As in some previous cases, calculation of the returns on the total fund without the derivatives or the incremental return would not be meaningful and is thus not recommended.

Appendix C. Model Request-for-Proposal Questions

The following model request-for-proposal (RFP) questions may be used by consultants, plan sponsors, and others in soliciting investment results and by investment managers in responding to such requests. The questions are intended to enable investment managers that claim compliance with the AIMR-PPS standards to report performance in compliance with the Standards when responding to RFPs and to enable issuers of RFPs to receive performance data that are in compliance with the Standards. Use of these questions will provide concise, consistent performance data, resulting in improved efficiencies and enhanced awareness of the AIMR-PPS standards. Requesters may choose to use some or all of these questions.

1. Performance Report:

   1a. Using the following format, please provide annual performance on a total-return basis from inception for the subject product. Use the AIMR Performance Presentation Standards (AIMR-PPS™) or, if entering performance calculated by different standards, indicate explicitly how the calculations differ:

			Subject Product/Composite Performance			
Year	Total Return (percent)	Benchmark Return[a] (percent)	Number of Portfolios	Dispersion	Total Assets at End of Period ($ millions)	Percentage of Firm's Assets
19xx						
19xx						
19xx						
19xx						
19xx						
19xx						
19xx						
19xx						
19xx						
19xx						

	3 Years Ended 12/31/9x (percent)	5 Years Ended 12/31/9x (percent)	10 Years Ended 12/31/9x (percent)
Annualized Returns			
Product/composite			
Benchmark[a]			
Difference			

[a]Presentation of benchmark returns is not required.

1b. By year, please annotate the causes for the differences shown.

1c. Indicate whether returns are net or gross of management fees. If returns are net of fees, please also provide gross-of-fees returns. If gross-of-fees returns are not available, please provide an explanation and a description of the fees that have been applied. Also provide the fee schedule for the portfolios in the product/composite shown above.

1d. Include a list of firmwide composites available.

1e. Indicate whether the returns have been determined on a trade-date or settlement-date basis.

2. Compliance with the AIMR-PPS standards:

2a. Is the firm in compliance with the AIMR-PPS standards? If not, please explain in what way the firm is not in compliance.

2b. Has a Level I (firmwide) verification been performed on the firm's portfolio composites? Was the firm found to be in compliance at this level? If not, please explain why. Are you taking steps to resolve deficiencies?

2c. Has a Level II (composite-specific) verification been performed on the composite shown in Question 1a? Was the composite found to be in compliance at this level? If not, please explain why. Are you taking steps to resolve deficiencies?

2d. Please provide the name and type of third party that performed the verification(s) and include a copy of the verification report.

3. Please provide an explanation for any noncompliance of performance periods, changes in name or ownership, or other exception to the AIMR-PPS standards.

4. Do you regularly reconcile individual portfolio returns to the records of the custodian(s) or client(s)? Please explain how often.

5. Discuss any performance attribution models or methodologies you use to analyze the sources of portfolio returns and value added. Please provide any attribution analysis of value-added returns versus the benchmark.

6. Please state the normal dispersion of investment results across client accounts for this product. State the reason for the dispersion.

7. What is the most appropriate benchmark to use in comparing your investment portfolios? Explain the choice.

The following suggested revised or new questions require more detail or different information from the information required in the previous questions.

For International Portfolios

1c. Indicate whether returns are net or gross of management fees. If returns are net of fees, please also present gross-of-fees returns. If gross-of-fees returns are not available, please provide an explanation and a description of the fees that have been applied. Specifically indicate whether the returns are net of all withholding taxes and taxes or potential taxes on realized and unrealized gains.

1f. Please disclose whether the actual portfolio is invested in countries that are outside the benchmark. Provide the location, type, and extent of these investments.

3. Please disclose how the exchange rates used in the calculations have been determined. Provide an explanation for any exceptions to this approach.

For Currency Overlay Portfolios

3. Please indicate whether the composite presented in the response to Question 1a is a single portfolio. Also disclose the number of performance composites the firm calculates.

For Real Estate Portfolios

1a. [Modify the format to include performance by income and appreciation.]

1c. Indicate whether returns are net or gross of management fees. If returns are net of fees, please provide an explanation of why gross-of-fees calculations are not available and a description of the fees that have been applied. Please disclose the management fee structure and its relationship to asset valuation.

1e. Indicate whether the income component is the net operating income or the income returned to investors.

8. Please provide your policy for property appraisals and valuations. If independent Member of Appraisal Institute appraisals are not performed on a regular basis for all properties in the composites, explain why.

9. Please provide your accounting policies for capital expenditures, free rent, leasing commissions, and tenant improvements.

For Portfolios Using Leverage and/or Derivatives

1e. Please describe the character, frequency, use, and extent of any and all derivatives-based strategies.

1f. If leverage has been used in the portfolio/composite, please provide the returns requested in Question 1a on an all-cash basis. If these returns are not available, please provide an explanation.

For Taxable Portfolios

1e. Please provide the tax rates assumed.

1f. Please indicate the timing of implied taxes on income and realized capital gains.

1g. Please indicate adjustments made for nondiscretionary capital withdrawals.

Appendix D. Sample Presentations

Presentation 1. XYZ Investment Firm Performance Results: Growth-plus-Income Balanced Composite, January 1, 1986, through December 31, 1995

Year	Total Return (percent)	Benchmark Return[a] (percent)	Number of Portfolios	Composite Dispersion (percent)	Total Assets at End of Period ($ millions)	Percentage of Firm Assets
1986	12.1	9.4	6	3.2	$50	80
1987	24.2	26.4	10	5.4	85	82
1988	17.0	16.4	15	3.8	120	78
1989	−3.3	−1.7	14	1.2	100	80
1990	15.8	12.8	18	4.3	124	75
1991	16.0	14.1	26	4.5	165	70
1992	2.2	1.8	32	2.0	235	68
1993	22.4	24.1	38	5.7	344	65
1994	7.1	6.0	45	2.8	445	64
1995	8.5	8.0	48	3.1	520	62

[a]*Editor's note*: Presentation of benchmark returns is not required.

XYZ Investment Firm has prepared and presented this report in compliance with the Performance Presentation Standards of the Association for Investment Management and Research (AIMR-PPS™). AIMR has not been involved with the preparation or review of this report.

Notes:
1. XYZ Investment Firm is a balanced portfolio investment manager that invests soley in U.S.-based securities. XYZ Investment Firm is defined as an independent investment management firm that is not affiliated with any parent organization.
2. These results have been prepared and presented in compliance with the AIMR-PPS standards only for the period January 1, 1990, through December 31, 1995. The full period is not in compliance. Prior to January 1, 1990, not all fully discretionary portfolios were represented in appropriate composites. Composite results for the years 1986 through 1989 include the five largest institutional portfolios that were managed in accordance with the growth-plus-income strategy. These five accounts are consistently represented in the composite for the full period from 1986 through 1989.
3. Results for the full historical period are time weighted. From 1986 through 1992, results were calculated yearly and the composites were asset weighted by beginning-of-year asset values. Since January 1, 1993, composites have been valued quarterly and portfolio returns have been weighted by using beginning-of-quarter market values plus weighted cash flows.
4. The benchmark: 60 percent S&P 500 Index; 40 percent Lehman Intermediate Aggregate Index. Annualized compound composite return = 11.9 percent; annualized compound benchmark return = 11.4 percent.
5. None of XYZ Investment Firm's balanced portfolio segments are included in any single-asset composites for the firm, and cash has been allocated evenly among asset segments.
6. Standard deviation in annual composite returns = 8.24 percent versus a standard deviation in the yearly benchmark returns of 8.53 percent.
7. The dispersion of annual returns is measured by the range between the highest- and lowest-performing portfolios in the composite.
8. Performance results are presented before management and custodial fees. The management fee schedule is attached.

9. No alteration of composites as presented here has occurred because of changes in personnel or other reasons at any time.
10. Settlement-date accounting was used prior to 1992.
11. A complete list of firm composites and performance results is available upon request.

Presentation 2. XYZ Investment Firm Supplemental Performance Results: Segment Returns for Medium-Risk Balanced Composite, 1993 and 1994

Composite	Total Return (percent)	Equity-Only Return (percent)	Fixed-Income-Only Return (percent)	Cash-Only Return (percent)
1994 return	5.2	5.0	6.1	3.3
Percentage of assets	100.0	45.0	45.0	10.0
1993 return	19.5	29.4	15.2	5.5
Percentage of assets	100.0	44.0	36.0	20.0

Presentation 3. XYZ Realty Fund I Historical Performance, 1988–95

Year	Net Assets (millions)	Income or Loss	Appreciation/ Depreciation	Total Gross Return
1988[a]	$175	7.0%	0.0%	7.0%
1989	194	9.0	4.0	13.3
1990	189	8.9	4.8	14.0
1991	194	8.4	2.8	11.4
1992	199	7.2	1.4	8.7
1993	195	7.4	−1.4	5.9
1994	203	6.5	0.8	7.3
1995	193	5.3	−9.0	−4.0

[a]Partial (three-quarters) year.

Notes:
1. Returns do not include annual investment management fee of 1 percent of gross asset value.
2. Assets are appraised annually by an independent Member of the Appraisal Institute appraiser.
3. Income is based on accrual accounting and recognized at the commingled fund level.
4. Returns include interest income from short-term cash investments.
5. Returns are based on audited operating results.
6. Returns presented are net of leverage, which averaged 30 percent of asset value during 1995.
7. All properties of XYZ Realty Fund I have been included in this performance presentation.
8. The sum of the income return component and appreciation return component may not equal the total gross return because of the time weighting of component quarterly returns.

Appendix E. AIMR Performance Presentation Standards Implementation Committee and Subcommittees

Implementation Committee: Lee N. Price, CFA, Co-Chair, RCM Capital Management; R. Charles Tschampion, CFA, Co-Chair, General Motors Investment Management Corporation; Thomas S. Drumm, CFA, Needham, MA; James E. Hollis III, CFA, Standish, Ayer & Wood, Inc.; James L. Kermes, Glenmede Trust; Dean S. Meiling, CFA, Pacific Investment Management Company; Ronald D. Peyton, Callan Associates; Robert E. Pruyne, Scudder, Stevens & Clark, Inc.; Neil E. Riddles, CFA, Templeton Global Investors, Inc.; Paul J. Silvester, CFA, State of Connecticut, Office of the Treasurer; John C. Stannard, CFA, Frank Russell Company Ltd.; George W. Weber, Frank Russell Investment Management Company. *SEC Observers*: Paul B. Goldman; Robert Zweig. *Observer*: Thomas Vock, CFA, Zurich Insurance Company. *AIMR Staff*: Michael S. Caccesse, Esquire; Edward W. Karppi; Pauline A. Pilate.

Bank Trust Subcommittee: James L. Kermes, Chair, Glenmede Trust; Richard M. Crouse, CFA, Pittsburgh National Bank; Jan A. Koenig, CFA, Bank South, N.A.; Catherine M. O'Connor, Bankers Trust Company.

Global PPS Subcommittee: Lee N. Price, CFA, Chair, RCM Capital Management; Carl Bacon, J.P. Morgan Investments; Ralf Bendheim, Deutscher Investment Trust; Louis Boulanger, William M. Mercer, Ltd.; Jonathan P. Buckeridge, Morgan Stanley Asset Management; James E. Hollis III, CFA, Standish, Ayer & Wood, Inc.; Ole Jacobsen, Unibank; Jan de Jonge, El Dorn, Netherlands; Prof. Dr. Otto Loistl, Wirtschaftsuniversitat Wien, Institut fur Finanzierung und Finanzmarkte; George W. Long, CFA, Long Investment Management Ltd.; David M. MacKendrick, EFFAS, Hampshire, UK; Iain W. McAra, Baring Asset Management; Neil E. Riddles, CFA, Templeton Global Investors, Inc.; John A. Rogers, Investments Analysts' Society of South Africa; John C. Stannard, CFA, Frank Russell Company; John R. Thomas, CFA, J.P. Morgan Trust Bank Ltd. (Tokyo); R. Charles Tschampion, CFA, General Motors Investment Management Corporation; Thomas Vock, CFA, Zurich Insurance Company. *Observer*: Alan Thomas, Investment Management Regulatory Organization.

Leverage/Derivatives Subcommittee: R. Charles Tschampion, CFA, Chair, General Motors Investment Management Corporation; Jeffrey A. Geller, CFA, BEA Associates; William P. Miller, CFA, General Motors Investment Management Corporation; J. Paula Pierce, Esquire, Commodities Corporation (USA); John C. Stannard, CFA, Frank Russell Company; Jeffrey L. Winter, CFA, QuantiLogic Asset Management Company.

Real Estate Subcommittee: Ronald Peyton, Chair, Callan Associates; Philip J. Lukowski, Heitman Financial Ltd.; Steven B. McSkimming, Institutional Property Consultants, Inc.; Paul S. Saint-Pierre, Institutional Real Estate Clearing House.

Taxable Portfolios Subcommittee: Lee N. Price, CFA, Co-Chair, RCM Capital Management; Robert E. Pruyne, Co-Chair, Scudder, Stevens & Clark, Inc.; Jean L.P. Brunel, CFA, Morgan Guaranty Trust Company of New York; Robert H. Jeffrey, The Jeffrey Company; Catherine O'Connor, Bankers Trust Company; John R. O'Toole, CFA, Mellon Equity Associates; Douglas S. Rogers, CFA, Heartland Adviser.

Venture and Private Placements Subcommittee: R. Charles Tschampion, CFA, Chair, General Motors Investment Management Corporation; T. Bondurant French, CFA, Brinson Partners, Inc.; Gail Marmorstein Sweeney, CFA, Cattanach & Associates; William P. Miller, CFA, General Motors Investment Management Corporation; Paul W. Price, CFA, State Street Bank and Trust Company; Jesse E. Reyes, Venture Economics.

Verification Subcommittee: Dean S. Meiling, CFA, Chair, Pacific Investment Management Company; DeWitt F. Bowman, CFA, Pension Investment Consulting; Matthew Forstenhausler, Ernst & Young; James E. Hollis III, CFA, Standish, Ayer & Wood, Inc.; Linda H. Ianieri, Coopers & Lybrand; Iain W. McAra, Baring Asset Management, Inc.; Stephen L. Nesbitt, Wilshire Associates, Inc.; Lawrence M. Unrein, AT&T Investment Management Corporation. *Observer*: Eric Felton, Arthur Anderson.

Wrap Fee Subcommittee: Thomas S. Drumm, CFA, Co-Chair, Needham, MA; Michael S. Caccese, Esquire, Co-Chair, AIMR; Steven M. Appledorn, CFA, Munder Capital Management, Inc.; David T. Ferrier, CFA, Merrill Lynch Consulting Services; Karen S. McCue, CFA, NWQ Investment Management Company; Christine D. Rose, Neuberger & Berman. *SEC Observer*: Robert E. Plaze.

Glossary

Absolute risk: See *Total risk*.

Aggregate return: Process of combining composite assets and cash flows to calculate performance as if the composite were one portfolio.

Asset-weighted return: Process of weighting the contributions to the composite rate of return by the beginning market values of the composite's constituent portfolios.

Beta: Measure of the sensitivity (volatility) of a composite's returns relative to its benchmark (index) return. Beta attempts to determine whether the composite is incurring more (or less) risk relative to the benchmark.

Cash flow: Difference between the number of dollars that came in and the number that went out of a portfolio.

Composite: Aggregation of individual portfolios or asset classes representing a similar investment objective or strategy.

Equal-weighted return: Simple averaging of performance for all the portfolios in a composite regardless of size.

Europe/Australia/Far East (EAFE) Index: Widely used index of non-U.S. stocks computed by Morgan Stanley Capital International.

Generally accepted accounting principles (GAAP): Common set of standards and procedures by which audited financial statements are prepared.

Guaranteed investment contract (GIC): Contract promising a stated nominal rate of interest over some specific time period, usually several years.

Index: Publicly available independent representation of the market.

Internal rate of return (IRR): Annualized implied discount rate calculated from a series of cash flows. IRR is the return that equates the present value of all invested capital in an investment to the present value of all returns or the discount rate that will provide a net present value of all cash flows equal to zero.

Market risk: Risk defined as the volatility of returns relative to the market or some other benchmark. Market risk addresses the pattern of returns relative to the market over time.

Multiple-asset portfolio: Portfolio that consists of more than one asset class.

One-on-one presentation: The U.S. Securities and Exchange Commission (SEC) defines one-on-one presentation as a manager performance presentation to any client, prospective client, consultant, or affiliated group entrusted to consider manager selection and retention.

Risk: See *Market risk, Total risk,* or *Risk measures.*

Relative risk: See *Market risk.*

Risk measures: Measures of the risk level of investment strategies, including standard deviation across time, beta, duration, and others that are based on current and historical data.

Sharpe measure: Measure of the total risk of a composite that includes the standard deviation of returns rather than considering only systematic risk by using beta. The ratio is the rate of return earned above the risk-free rate to the standard deviation of the portfolio.

Standard deviation: Measure of the variability (dispersion) of historical returns around their central tendency (mean return). Standard deviation attempts to measure how much exposure to volatility was taken historically by the implementation of an investment strategy.

Systematic risk: See *Market risk.*

Total risk: Variability of actual (absolute) returns rather than variability relative to the market. Total risk addresses the absolute returns over time.

Treynor measure: Ratio of the rate of return earned above the risk-free rate to the portfolio beta during the time period under consideration.

Vintage year: Date of the first directed capital contribution.

Volatility measures: Measures indicating the risk of having returns different from a particular benchmark or index; the total variability of actual returns.

Wrap-fee account: The SEC definition is "a program [account] in which any client is charged a specific fee or fees not based directly upon transactions in a client's account for investment advisory services (which may include portfolio management or advice concerning the selection of other investment advisers) and execution of client transactions."

Index

F

G

H

I

L

M